BASIC PRINCIPLES FOR SOCIAL SCIENCE
IN OUR TIME

BASIC PRINCIPLES FOR SOCIAL SCIENCE IN OUR TIME

edited, with an introduction by

Kenneth Westhues

UNIVERSITY OF ST. JEROME'S COLLEGE PRESS
1987

BASIC PRINCIPLES FOR SOCIAL SCIENCE
IN OUR TIME

Canadian Cataloguing in Publication Data
Main entry under title:

Basic principles for social science in our time

Proceedings of the Conference on Basic Principles for
Social Science in Our Time, held in May 1986, in
Kitchener and Waterloo, Ont.
Includes bibliographies.
ISBN 0-9693048-0-3

1. Social sciences – Philosophy – Congresses.
I. Westhues, Kenneth. II. Conference on Basic
Principles for Social Science in Our Time (1986 :
Kitchener and Waterloo, Ont.).

H61.B38 1987   300'.1   C87-0984620-X

Cover design by Kate Groves
Typeset by Virginia L. Freeman MacOwan

Printed in Canada

CONTENTS

Context and Introduction: The Social Fact   1

PART I: ACCEPTANCE OF HUMAN AGENCY   37

1   On the Social Construction of Knowledge   38
    Kenneth J. Gergen

2   A Plea for the Categories   53
    David MacGregor

PART II: MORAL ENGAGEMENT   65

3   A Typology of Intellectuals   66
    Christopher Lasch

4   Humanist Sociology: Scientific and Critical   77
    Gregory Baum

5   Social Science as Moral Inquiry   92
    Yi-Fu Tuan

6   Toward a Humanist History of Sex   104
    Serge Gagnon

PART III: PRACTICALITY   117

7   Social Sciences, Human Survival, Development and
    Liberation   118
    David G. Gil

8   Can There Be a Humanist Social Science?   130
    Shoukry T. Roweis

Appendix: Ten Classic Guides   148
Afterword of Thanks   150
Notes on Contributors   151

As Dante instructs us in *The Divine Comedy*, "Consider your origins. You were not made to live like creatures lesser than yourselves, but to follow the ways of both knowledge and virtue." In my mind, to heed that instruction is to apprehend what is the most basic principle for social science–in this or any other time.

GREGORY SORBARA,
Minister of Colleges and Universities, Government of Ontario, in his address to the conference on "Basic Principles for Social Science in Our Time," Kitchener, May 4, 1986

CONTEXT AND INTRODUCTION:
THE SOCIAL FACT

Kenneth Westhues

With collegial best wishes, this book is addressed before all to young social scientists, those just completing their degrees and beginning their careers. You are entering an industry that, by census classification, embraces about two percent of the labour force of the industrialized Western world. You are part of a huge and distinctive institution of our society, however little you may have thought of it. For you have probably identified yourself mainly with a particular profession or specialty– with psychology, history, sociology, planning, geography, political science, social work, or whatever. One purpose of this book is to heighten your awareness of social science as a whole, so that you can play your special part successfully, effectively, and responsibly. The authors of the eight chapters herein, all of which are easy to read and understand, work in seven different fields. Reading their words, you will gain a broader vision, a perspective within which to see more clearly what you are doing. Collectively, these authors will bring home to you the fact that which social science you practice matters less than how you practice it, and less than anyone might guess, given how separate the degree programs, professional associations, and career patterns have become.

The further purpose of this book is to recommend to you certain basic principles for the success of your life's work. Not *all* such principles. We hardly pretend to have captured in these pages every idea that is basic to social science, only some of the most essential, relevant and timely ones. Nor do the principles offered here take the form of a tidy list or tightly logical system. Lists, systems, formulas and recipes have a place in social science, to be sure–as they do in any line of work, from cooking to child-rearing. The most basic and important principles, however, the ones that make the difference between stultifying mediocrity and surprising excellence, are notoriously resistant to precise formulation and open to diverse phraseologies. Often they must be read *between* lines of prose, or even grasped intuitively while watching a great practitioner at work. This book is not a take-it-or-leave-it package of meaning for your occupation, but some interwoven strands of thought that will help you define a meaning of your own.

The chapters that follow are the authors' respective answers to the question, "What do *you* consider the most basic principles for social science in our time?" This was the question I posed in inviting them to speak at a conference held in Kitchener-Waterloo, Canada, in 1986. Eleven of us senior professors in the three adjacent universities (St. Jerome's, Waterloo, Wilfrid Laurier) had formed ourselves into a committee and decided to host the conference. As committee chair, I had surveyed the other members, asking who in their judgment could offer trustworthy principles for doing the work of social science well. From that survey came the names of those invited to take part, in particular the 13 individuals from whom formal papers were solicited. This little book is hardly a full report on what was, by common estimation, an extraordinary intellectual event.[1] It is instead an outcome of the conference: an introductory statement of context and summary, then a coherent sequence of eight papers, and finally an appendix of recommended classic works. This introduction is my effort to capture the collective sense of the conference in a form that will be useful to a new generation of social scientists. But though it relies on the thought of 160 conference participants and on a sizable literature, this rendition of basic principles comes from my particular pen. The best ideas, I should repeat, are subject to diverse phraseologies.

One final preliminary point bears mention. The authors of the chapters that follow are themselves successful social scientists. This is not to imply that a philosopher of science, for instance, a novelist or undergraduate student is incapable of insight about how to practice social science well. Indeed, one of the principles recurrent in these chapters is that we credentialed academics should listen more closely and respectfully to the uncredentialed voices altogether outside academic life. Nonetheless, it is reassuring to hear this and other principles from scholars who have held prominent professorships and prestigious fellowships, who are quoted in the public press, who have been awarded honorary degrees, who have written many books, and whose books have won awards and been translated into many languages. No advice should be weighed so carefully as that given by people who themselves excel in the relevant activity. I can therefore recommend these chapters with some confidence, even as I count it an honour to introduce them.

The Social Fact

In his widely influential *Rules of Sociological Method*,[2] Emile Durkheim urged the study of "social facts," established beliefs and practices that bear down on people from above and compel their conformity. But most social facts, however demonstrable in certain societies in certain periods, are rather less factual than Durkheim seemed to think. They are not universal and they do not last. We in social science are students of fluid facts. The beliefs and practices we observe are fleeting moments in a process of establishing and disestablishing. Heraclitus has warned us: if we observe the exact same river twice, we need to have our methods checked.

In a singular sense, however, the social fact is the first principle of social science–the fact, as John Donne put it, that "no man is an island, entire of itself."[3] Nobody's body is simply his or hers. Self-made millionaires are fantasies. All psychology is *social* psychology. Vertebrate anatomy aside, there is nothing to study in a human being except evidence of relationships between him or her and other people (and the act of studying is a further relationship). These ties between people do not change overnight. They cling endlessly, moreover, each one leaving indelible marks upon the biographies of all involved. In a provisory way, one can indeed analyze John Doe or Mary Smith as if they were separately real. At any given point in the brief individual lifetime, every human has a more or less stable identity or personality, distinguishable from others and describable in this way or that. But human life, the subject-matter of social science, is not a mass of variously shaped specimens spilling out over time like gravel from a dumptruck. It is *in fact* the relations among people across and within the generations, the relations also between people and the natural environment of earth.

The implications of the social fact for social scientists are vast, giving spice to our work especially in societies where individual liberty is a key value and where individual rights are the very basis of political and economic organization. The social fact by no means obliges us to oppose private property, free enterprise or competitive elections, much less to work at curtailing the cherished freedoms citizens here enjoy. How much individual self-assertion is beneficial in work organization, economic exchange, marriage, schools or wherever is a matter for informed and reasoned debate, and there is no single right answer. We are obliged, however, in our papers and presentations, to get across the essential point: that individual liberty and rights are not absolutes but artifacts of social order, derivations from the social bond, products of the historical process.[4] My freedom of speech depends on the language others taught me. My freedom of movement depends on others' production of cars and planes. No one behaves freely except in the context of relationships that allow as much. This is the fact honesty requires us to convey in our social scientific work.

The social fact has more immediate implications as well, since we social scientists are ourselves human beings. Our occupation does not emancipate us from the social bond. However much we study the human species, we still belong to it–and to a particular experiment in how it can be organized. Indeed, who we are as social scientists is a function of how we are related to other people: forebears, contemporaries, progeny. Detachment is not an option. It is a question of what kind of relations we maintain with whom, and of how aware of them we are. From the start of a career until its end, you probe and ponder whose ox is being gored by your work, and whose is being fed. For you are not after all just making a career. Years pass. Over and over you extract from the word processor some pages called a *vita*: your life, no less.

Two critical kinds of relationship are addressed briefly in the following pages: those between the social scientific community and the larger society, and between this community and its constituent professions, the established disciplines. Inspection of these relationships must rest, however, on a clear conception of the social scientific enterprise. This is sketched immediately below.

Social science

The basic difference between social scientists and most other people in the labour force is that we deal in words while they deal in physical goods and services. Both they and we produce, maintain, overhaul and distribute something. But the object of their labour is empirically real: the material substance of the current way of life, whether tangible goods like food and clothing or services like haircuts and car repair. By contrast, the object of our labour is only mentally real: the ideas set forth in our lectures, colloquia, theses, papers, reports, articles and books. Tangible goods like libraries and computers play a part in what we do, and our research may require various physical skills. Contrariwise, words are involved in other people's jobs. In our case, however, the material realities are for the sake of words. In their case it is the other way around. Our occupation is defined by its purely symbolic output: the preservation and revision of old ideas, the formulation of new ones.

In the rarefied atmosphere of universities and research bureaucracies, it is easy to overlook the fact that the vast majority of working citizens, even in the industrialized Western world, do physically productive work.[5] The standard of living requires as much. About half of the Canadian or American paid labour force still consists of farmers and blue-collar workers. Further, at least half of white-collar workers do something more than talk and push a pen: letter carriers, for instance, sales clerks, stock clerks, counter clerks, surgeons, dentists, technicians of various kinds, typists and operators of other office machines. Physically productive work occupies also the millions of women outside the paid labour force whose days are spent in the care of children and maintenance of the home. We social scientists, in sum, belong to that remarkably small minority of working adults—perhaps 15 or 20 percent—whose contribution to life in common is nothing more than words.

Even among people who talk and write for a living, we are distinguished by how abstract and general our words are, how far removed from tangible goods and physical services. An insurance agent merely listens, talks and writes, but with crucial practical consequences when a claim is made. A sales representative talks up particular goods so well that the goods change hands. Managers and administrators are defined by their words of decision about how specific resources will be used. The numbers that accountants, bookkeepers, and bank tellers record and manipulate are not nearly so abstract as they appear, representing as they do what the holders of accounts can and cannot buy. In contrast to the words of all these other white-collar workers, ours point not to particular people or goods, but always to some general pattern, principle or rule, which may or may not be relevant to the handling of a given case. A social scientist's decision-making power, moreover, extends only to the conduct of his or her own cerebral work, and perhaps that of a small research staff.

The distance of words from concrete issues also distinguishes social scientists proper from those in applied or related fields. A social case-worker, lawyer, or probation officer deals with *this* client, a school psychologist with *this* child, a market researcher with *this* product, a public opinion pollster with *this* survey on *this* issue, an urban planner with *this* neighbourhood, a community developer with *this* identified need, and so on through a long list of occupations. These practitioners act on many bases, including common sense, personal experience, political exigencies, hunches, and bluff. Presumably they also act in some degree on the basis of what we social scientists have communicated *in general terms* through our courses, seminars, reports, articles and books.

The point at which social science shades off into related fields is, of course, imprecise. A journalist who writes simple factual reports of newsworthy happenings is seldom called a social scientist. Yet the term properly applies to a Gwynne Dyer or George Will, writing interpretations of events in light of some theory of society. Walter Lippmann is appropriately biographized in the *International Encyclopedia of the Social Sciences*. Similarly, an historian who merely chronicles successions of events probably resists being called a social scientist. So, too, a professor of social work whose teaching revolves around immediate practical issues and skills. But more theoretical historians (like Charles Beard, Arnold Toynbee, and Richard Hofstadter) and analysts of social welfare (like Jane Addams, Sidney and Beatrice Webb) rank among the major social scientists of this century. What distinguishes our occupation from closely allied ones is abstraction from immediate events, particular people, specific goods, and everyday practical affairs. Distance is the hallmark of the words of a social scientist.

For clarifying our location in the web of relationships that constitutes human life, we can distinguish ourselves from two other kinds of producers of distant words. First are the natural scientists, those who speak and write in general terms about all that is not distinctly human—the chemists, biologists, physicists, astronomers, geologists and so on. Their subject matter lacks a mind of its own. It cannot be an audience or readership for the scientists' words, nor act in response to those words. It is far less varied than human phenomena, and changes far less rapidly. What natural scientists study is the human environment, the given and inescapable context for the diverse projects of the human species. Especially during the past century, natural scientists have come up with theories incredibly useful for achieving human purposes, from disease prevention to space exploration. By now, massive funding of natural scientific research is institutionalized. By a kind of halo effect, we social scientists also benefit. The trouble is that we have not yet produced any theories of unquestioned usefulness. Whether our words have eased social ills like poverty, crime, war, family breakdown, unemployment and political demagoguery is highly debatable. We have not discovered an effective cure for even one such ill. Studying a subject matter that talks back and repeatedly transforms itself puts us in quite a different ballgame.[6]

Finally are those whose words are distant from practical realities but intrinsically valuable for the way they are put together. If flowers can be beautifully arranged, if this is in itself worthwhile, ought not the same be true of words? And so there are poets, novelists, playwrights, humourists, singers, actors—and professors who teach and write about the art of language use. This is not to say that literature is free of implications for action. On the contrary, every work of it betrays the social context of its author and recommends certain behaviours even if implicitly. But its purpose is to delight and entertain, indeed to lift readers or listeners out of immediate practicalities and affirm their ability to transcend experience. The contribution of storytellers and similar artists to the collective good is not hard to understand.

But again, the ballgame of social scientists is of a different kind. Rarely are we accused of writing beautiful prose, much less poetry. Nor is this our chief aim, however carefully we polish our spoken and written work. Our words, so we insist, are valuable not for their beauty but for their fit with human life as it generally has been lived. This is what the empirical method means: that we make our sentences square with the realities of life in some society. Many literary artists have managed this as well—George Orwell, for instance, Upton Sinclair, John Steinbeck. Among social scientists, however, accuracy outranks beauty as a measure of the worth of words.[7]

Clearly, then, we social scientists labour in a highly unusual way. The maintenance of the present way of life requires the vast majority of able-bodied citizens to do physically productive work. Most of those who get to talk or write their way through life must nonetheless tie their words closely to the work of production and immediate concerns. We, however, are exempt. We get to speak and write in generalities. Our words are not weighed for their beauty, nor for their insight into the natural environment of earth. To be a social scientist is to work at learning, preserving, revising, formulating, and communicating general ideas that square with some observable, distinctly human reality. It is hard to imagine an occupation more privileged, even laying aside the above-average incomes we enjoy. The question is why we spend our lives this way, why our society allows us to. If relationships are the stuff of human life, and if we ourselves are human beings, then how do we relate to everybody else?

Social science and society

"The author wishes to thank especially the untold numbers of Canadian taxpayers who assure the financing of universities and granting bodies."[8] So reads the first sentence of a book by Serge Gagnon, author of Chapter 6 in the present volume. His sentiment points to the most obvious relation between us and our fellow citizens, namely, that they provide us with our livelihoods. They do this in greatest part through taxes paid to various levels of government, since the paycheques of the vast majority of us come mainly from public funds. We are supported also by students' tuition fees, consulting and lecture fees paid by businesses and private organizations, and royalties paid by purchasers of books. Our first duty is therefore to reject any suggestion of the autonomy or self-sufficiency of our work, to acknowledge our own dependence on the social fact. In Chapter 3 herein, Christopher Lasch highlights this duty, and the need to maintain the posture of gratitude apparent in the quote above from Gagnon.

For repaying the people who foot our bills, all we as social scientists can offer is words. A word of thanks first of all, and beyond this, words they can use for improving the quality of the various relationships in which they are involved. The occasions for doing this are varied: academic courses, articles in newspapers and magazines, lectures and books aimed at various publics, consultancies to organizations of whatever kind. One way for us to repay debts is to give people in or preparing for occupations more practical than ours knowledge that will enable them to relate more effectively and responsibly to the people they serve at work. This is what it means to teach social science in a faculty of law, planning, medicine, social work, business or education, or to address practitioners in these fields. No less worthwhile is the communication of knowledge useful to others in their dealings even beyond the workplace: in marriage and family, friendship and club, church and union, and above all the civic community. This is what it means to teach social science in a faculty of arts, and to join orally or in print the debates on current public issues. We social scientists have an opportunity denied to nearly everybody else, namely to observe and ponder at length and in detail the varied ways of human life and the varied outcomes attached thereto. The test of whether we are worth our salt is whether we can offer other people more helpful ideas than they can think up on their own during coffee breaks.

We can fail this test in lots of ways. One is to discriminate in the offering of our words, giving them selectively to the more powerful of our fellow citizens, and contributing thereby to dominative, dehumanizing relationships. The usefulness of our ideas then consists in strengthening the hold of elites on other people's lives. In great part, this is precisely what we do. The students we teach are disproportionately from the advantaged classes. Most of the jobs for which we prepare them, moreover, are marked by relationships wherein the job incumbent exercises more power over other people than they do over him or her. What else does it mean to be a manager, or indeed a professional insulated by scarce knowledge from the countervailing power of patients or clients? Our discrimination in favour of elites is apparent also in the fact that far more social scientific lectures, reports and consultancies are directed to representatives of capital (the management of business firms, for instance, or think-tanks bankrolled by large corporations) than to people in the working class. This is hardly surprising, since the former control more funds with which to pay for words, and have more time to listen.

To whom we talk, of course, conditions what we say. In so far as our dialogue is mainly with advantaged classes and elites, our tendency is to offer knowledge that in one way or another justifies their dominative positions and retards progressive change.[9] We conjure up explanations of the way things are that rule out even the possibility of things being otherwise. We portray the structure of life at hand as a natural fact, instead of as one evanescent historical expression of the much broader social fact. Virtually all the chapters in this book are directed against this kind of social science, the kind that only buttresses the established imbalances of power. From Kenneth Gergen's insistence on the social construction of knowledge in Chapter 1, to Shoukry Roweis's attack on totalization in Chapter 8, you will confront reminders that an adequate social science is not a wintery freeze of the status quo, but a spring-like affirmation of new possibilities.

To take from the collective product of this and previous societies, but to return useful words mainly to elites, is to fail not just as a social scientist but as a human being. Among forms of failure, however, this is not the one to which we are currently most disposed. For most of us teach in colleges and universities. We give words mainly in academic lectures, and it is hard to say what effect they have on anything. Most of our students are months, even years removed from the practice of occupations, as well as from most other adult responsibilities. How much of what we say do they hear, much less remember, still less act upon? To be sure, students jump the hoops set as degree requirements. Their degrees do matter–for both job prospects and prestige.[10] But one can pass courses without learning in them or changing on account of them. Have you not done this yourself? Quite possibly, the content of most social-science courses is ultimately lost on most of the students enrolled.

Whatever doubts can be raised about the effect of classroom words, upon which students are tested, apply all the more to consultants' presentations, the recipients' grasp of which is not even formally assessed. In Canada, the royal commission is perhaps the grandest occasion for social scientists to offer knowledge to political elites and the public at large. Yet it is clear that royal commissions are often mere delaying tactics on the part of governments or excuses for inaction, and that many commission reports might as well have been given to the wind. This is the more true of research reports commissioned by particular ministries and lower-level agencies. The worry, in sum, is that we social scientists give our gifts of words mainly in contexts where most of them are not received, or if received are not accepted, or if accepted are nonetheless not put into practical effect.

Yet a bigger worry hangs over social science in our time, a third scenario of failure. It is the inordinate priority on exchanging words among ourselves, to the neglect of communicating at all with people outside our various fields. As a young social scientist, you know well that in most academic settings, an investment of your energy in good teaching, hard work at engaging your students and helping them learn, is not the best way to gain job security, promotion, or salary increments. A plunge into practical research and consultation with nonacademic organizations (except very elite ones) is no better. What counts above all is "contributions to scholarship," that is, papers presented at meetings of learned societies, articles in academic journals, and books of the kind that are reviewed in those same journals. These are the gifts of words that you put up front on your *curriculum vitae*, for these are the ones most valued by the committees that decide your occupational fate–committees composed almost entirely of social scientists like yourself. The words social scientists are most rewarded for are the ones they give to other social scientists.

Practitioners of any craft like to trade ideas, and it is necessary and good that they do so. They may also join to enforce standards of performance, to ensure a fair return for their work, and to promote basic and long-term research relevant to them. This, too, is legitimate and good. The question is whether we practitioners of social science are not so much occupied with talking among ourselves and so isolated from evaluation by outsiders, that we constitute a kind of parasitic community. We like to claim that ours are "young" sciences in need of more time to demonstrate the practical value apparent by now in physics or chemistry. We have indeed ridden the coattails of the natural sciences to our position of strength in the universities (that is one reason we call ourselves social *scientists*). We have played upon popular fears about social problems like poverty and crime to win research funds from the public purse. But ours is, after all, a different ballgame. Social scientists who spend their lives "contributing to knowledge," building great bodies of thought whose worth is to be apparent only on completion in 50 or 100 years, are probably not contributing to anything at all–beyond the success of their careers and the stagnation of the society at hand.

You can fail as a producer of words, even while moving up the income scale and enjoying a comfortable life. It comes down in the end to how much useful knowledge you somehow give to your fellow citizens in return for everything they give you. You will devise your own strategy for escaping failure, for contributing in an effective way without discrimination in favour of elites. If you work at it, you *can* become a teacher students will remember. By involving the organizations you serve in the planning and execution of research, by some adroit playing of politics, by skillful dealings with the media, and so on, you *can* ensure that your consultancies are taken seriously. By honing your writing skills, you *can* find a public readership for your articles and books. You can even, by the character of your scholarly contributions, nudge the social scientific community toward a posture of greater responsiveness to public issues (such, indeed, is the motive for this book). The strategy you follow must be your own, informed by your personal talents and areas of expertise, your values and theory of society, the job opportunities available to you, and the social situation in which you live. But two general points are worth keeping in mind, one intellectual and the other practical.

The crucial intellectual point is that empirical accuracy or adequacy must not be the sole criterion for deciding what to say or write.[11] To have drawn your sample, measured your variables, and tested your hypotheses carefully, to have accounted for 30 or 50 or 70 percent of the variance in some phenomenon–to have demonstrated, in sum, that your words do fit the data is not enough to make those words worth sharing with anyone. This may seem to be enough in an isolated little community of social scientists. You may get caught up in interminable debates about which theory explains the data best, which variables should or should not be added to some path diagram, and into how many subscales some overall scale should be factored. You may embark on the endless quest for definitive data, hunger for the chance to replicate your hypotheses cross-nationally, and end each of your articles with a call for more research. Method may indeed become your way of life, even if you are not formally a methodologist. All that will matter is that your words have more empirical support than the words someone else has put in print. And all that will result is pages of prose that confirm what ordinary people already know or that distract them from practical concerns.

"*Interesting*," Yi-Fu Tuan exclaims in Chapter 5 herein. "This word, by now, is one of the weakest in the English lexicon. Do we scholars labour for no greater aim than to produce something *interesting*?" Of course not. We labour to produce words that are at once empirically supported (hence "interesting" to methodologically inclined colleagues) and genuinely helpful to people outside our community. Empiricism in social research will make you a social scientist. Empiricism plus responsiveness to practical issues will make you a good one. Two distinct criteria must be applied to every idea you consider offering in a lecture or written work. First, does it square with current realities of life? Second, is this what most needs to be said, will it be useful to hearers or readers for transforming or transcending these realities? The world is full of ideas that are true, more or less consistent with observable facts. There is some truth in even rejected hypotheses. Within intellectual communities out of touch with everyday problems, one batch of true ideas comes into fashion, another goes out, much like hemlines on skirts. Our challenge is to choose or conjure up some true idea that responds to *these* people at *this* moment in *their particular* situation. Presenting "the latest research findings" is simply not enough.

The practical concluding point is that responsiveness to real human concerns may require you to put your social scientific work on hold from time to time and to involve yourself directly in practical affairs. Who knows what this might mean! Perhaps getting elected to public office, starting your own business, organizing a social movement, becoming an applied professional, or taking a job in some seemingly unrelated field. For if you do your science well, you will sooner or later settle upon some theory about life in this society or some part of it, a theory at once descriptive of how things have been until now, and suggestive of how they might be improved. You will test your theory empirically, not just in systematic investigations but in day-by-day reflection on personal experience, newspaper reports, whatever information reaches you. You will spell out your theory in spoken and written words. It will creep into your lectures, whatever the course, and your research reports, regardless of topic. But what then? Will you spend your (by then) tenured career filling in the details of your theory, presenting it to successive cohorts of students, testing it on still other data-sets? Your theory will undoubtedly improve over time. But over time you may also fall in love with your own words, mistake blueprint for building, revel in your solution of problems on paper as if they were thereby solved in fact. You might become in old age one of those charming, curmudgeonly intellectuals who has something interesting to say about everything, and who makes no difference in anything.

Among participants in the conference where the chapters of this book were read, the most noticeable division was not by discipline. It was not even an intellectual difference. The split was between scholars who are content to go on producing words, leaving the work of application to others, and those who mix in their own working lives the production of words and direct involvement in social practice. Each side could claim distinguished ancestors. Hegel, whose singular importance David MacGregor documents in Chapter 2, never ventured much outside the academy. Neither did Kant or Veblen. Nor in our day, Jürgen Habermas or Anthony Giddens. On the other, activist side stand Karl Marx (organizing workers), Benedetto Croce (opposing fascism in Italian politics), John Dewey (organizing professors, defending Trotsky), Jane Addams (founding Hull House), Lewis Mumford (working in urban design), and Michael Harrington (organizing socialist movements), among many others. The present volume represents both sides, from Gergen and MacGregor to Gil and Roweis. All would agree, however, that where you come down on this issue depends in greatest part on your own talents and the demands of the situation facing you. That a theorist should also be a direct practitioner is hardly a universal moral law. Yet this may be the best way for you to satisfy your debt to the social bond.

Social science and its divisions

Few social scientists pay allegiance to social science, or even think much about it. No one doubts that it exists–as a census and library classification, as the object of agencies that fund research, or as the organizing principle of distinct faculties in some universities. There is an obviously identifiable mass of knowledge that goes by this name. Witness the two English-language encyclopedias of the social sciences and the conferences regularly held on topics like "new directions in social science." There are even a few organizations explicitly aimed at promoting the field–the Social Science Federation of Canada, for example.

The word *federation* in that organization's name, however, says a lot. So does the fact that the plural, *social sciences*, is more commonly heard than the singular. Indeed, the most common way of defining the overall field is to list the particular subfields.[12] These latter are by far the most immediately relevant reality. University students study and get degrees only rarely in social science, more often in anthropology, planning, social work, recreation, or some other specific field. Professors think of themselves much less as social scientists than as sociologists, geographers, criminologists, political scientists, and so on. Few journals are identified with social science as a whole (these are mainly low-circulation curiosities), and the major ones are tied to particularities like psychology, economics, law, or education. The word *discipline* is ordinarily reserved for these subfields, while social science itself is reduced to the status of a supplementary *interdisciplinary* activity. The question is why.

To answer that these disciplines refer to separate bodies of knowledge is to confess and spread the ignorance of youth. I recall my panic as a graduate sociology student upon being assigned to take a course in anthropology, a field in which I had never taken even an undergraduate course. How could I possibly pass one at the graduate level? But of course I did pass it, with such distinction (so I discovered years later) that the professor published my research under his own name. The course was a valuable lesson in more ways than one. Year by year ever since, the falsity of intellectual boundaries between disciplines has been impressed on me steadily more. In this very book you will see psychologist Gergen's indebtedness to sociologists Peter Berger and Thomas Luckmann. For the title of Chapter 2, sociologist MacGregor adapts a line from economist Harold Innis, and the chapter itself is mainly about philosopher Georg Hegel. Historian Lasch dwells on sociologist C. Wright Mills and psychologist Melanie Klein. Geographer Tuan cites mainly anthropologists. Theologian Baum traces various influences upon him—Weber, Mannheim, the Frankfurt School. Historian Gagnon deals in sexology. The four footnotes in the chapter by social worker David Gil are to philosopher John Rawls, psychologist Abraham Maslow, educator Paolo Freire, and sometime journalist Karl Marx. Planning theorist Roweis roots the final chapter in the work of philosopher Michel Foucault. Where then are the boundaries, given that the variation in ideas produced within disciplines almost matches the variation between them?

The answer is no secret: the boundaries are in the organization of social scientists. Each discipline is more accurately a profession, an organized network of word producers who control, on the basis of their alleged special knowledge, a certain range of jobs. These jobs may be mainly in academic and research institutions (the case of history, sociology, or political science) or they may include both academic and applied positions (the case of law, social work, or planning). In either case, admission to the network requires at a minimum earning a degree from people already in it. The control over jobs may be enforced by law (increasingly the case in psychology) or simply by custom (as when job applicants who lack the normal credentials are routinely passed over). The key point is that social scientists are divided into a dozen or so large groups, each of which has succeeded over time in staking its claim to some number of jobs. This fundamentally is why the loyalty of social scientists goes to particular professions rather than to the overall field. The former, not the latter, buy your groceries and pay your rent.

This fact promotes not only dedication to one's own profession but distrust of the other ones. The obstacles to open, problem-centred scholarship include plain ignorance of how similar the various disciplines are but what is more important, the need to guard one's own disciplinary turf against competitors. The industry is structured, that is, very much as a zero-sum game among professions. Every new university professorship in anthropology diminishes the prospect of appointments in history. Should one expect a psychologist to admit how capably social workers or sociologists might fill jobs now reserved for psychologists? Is it in the interests of a planner to acknowledge how much of this field overlaps with economics and politics? Our situation in social science is not unique. In health science obstetricians fear midwives, family doctors are wary of nurse-practitioners, and prescribers of drugs disdain prescribers of vitamins. In many respects, professions in today's Western world are what local communities used to be: contexts of overwhelming importance to their members' livelihoods, hence objects of fanatic loyalty and wildly exaggerated claims of value and distinctiveness. However much well-schooled professionals grin at the narrowness of peasants in their separate villages, parochialism and professionalism are simply not that far apart.[13]

In a world more rational than ours, you would not begin your career as a producer of social scientific words by learning an established discipline. You would start with some real problem–maybe a social problem like poverty, voter apathy, sexual inequality, or environmental pollution, maybe a basic human problem like death or change. Then you would scrounge about for good ideas, following your nose to teachers, authors and colleagues regardless of what credentials they might have. You would test your ideas empirically, and try them out on the people you would hope to serve. With further reading, reflection, research and dialogue, you would over time give coherence to your thought and broaden it to other aspects of social life. By then you could look over your shoulder and see the discipline to which you would belong. It would be simply the body of assumptions, concepts, theories, findings and other ideas underlying the words from your own mouth and pen. In another sense, your discipline would consist of all those thinkers, past and present, sharing with you a commitment to that body of thought. And then, both as an independent scholar and as a member of this discipline, you would set about paying off your debt to the social bond.

As your own experience probably reflects, such a process happens even now to some extent. It is apparent also in the chapters of this book, none of whose authors is overmuch constrained by the boundaries of his profession. One can even fairly say that, despite their diverse professional starting points, these authors have by now made their individual ways to quite a common discipline. The words they separately produce run coherently in a more or less common vein. Albeit with varying accents, attributable as much to ethnicity and upbringing as to profession, they share a language and can speak productively with one another. Indeed they did so, along with scores of other scholars, at the conference where these chapters first were read.

But these scholars have more vision than most. Besides, their average age is about 55. They have tenure in their jobs. Their personal reputations are strong. They can afford to wear their professional identities lightly. The beginning social scientist cannot. The student may arrive on campus concerned about some real human problem but even in the introductory course he or she confronts a discipline already established, prepackaged, prefabricated by a profession through its local embodiment, the academic department or professional school. The student's initial, often practical concern is sometimes belittled ("So you want to change the world, do you?"). More often it is ignored, and the student simply immersed in the preordained curriculum. Gradually and understandably the student's perspective shifts. The name of the game is to understand not this problem, this society, or this uncertain human life, but sociology, economics, or some other supposedly special body of knowledge about human life. Absorbing the textbook truths, mastering the literature of the discipline, comes to take precedence over learning about life. For the latter will not likely secure a degree or job. What is required is high marks in a preset sequence of courses, a thesis that leaders of the profession rave about, and the kind of professional deportment that will ensure burbly letters of recommendation. The game changes little after commencement of salaried employment. Publication in the profession's journals, participation in its meetings, and collegial harmony with senior figures in this same profession are the keys to survival in your job. If lots of social scientists have tunnel vision, it is because they have been kept in tunnels for so long that even with tenure, they cannot find their way out.

But there is hope. The more conscious you become of how much the professions have fragmented and balkanized social science, the more able you will be to resist servitude to any one of them and to take control of your career. You will not then let your profession define your discipline, but you yourself will define it, in company with others of like mind. You may choose, for example, to work in one of the smaller colleges or universities, perhaps one with a denominational affiliation or other special character, if it offers colleagues who share your assumptions and can therefore help you produce the words you want to produce. These small institutions give probably the best schooling in social science available today, in part because their faculties are so small that members of various professions are obliged to talk to one another, read and evaluate each other's work, and respect each other's opinions. Professors in these mainly undergraduate colleges are often portrayed as scholars who "couldn't make it" in the prestigious graduate schools.[14] Such portrayal is unfairly broad. Many of them simply and wisely decided not to spend their lives churning out articles for professional journals that go largely unread outside the circles of those who write for them.

You may choose, on the other hand, to work altogether outside academic life, where social science is divided not so much by the professions as by topic of research or political orientation. Governmental research agencies typically care less about credentials in a particular established discipline than about general skills in research, writing, and personal relations, interest and expertise in a given area of public policy (like child welfare, unemployment, drug abuse, or urban development), and concurrence with the agency's political slant. The same goes for private research institutions and think-tanks, whether on the right or left. The point applies as well to the many thousands of newspapers and magazines in North America which have social scientists in their employ—as columnists, editorial writers, editors, but often in the first instance as reporters. There is also the tough option of writing books for public readerships: what matters to a trade editor is less the prospective author's degrees than how many people are likely to buy the prospective book.

Except for the few directly tied to an academic profession, nonacademic careers like these are rarely recommended to candidates for the M.A. or Ph.D. in social scientific fields. There is even a tendency to write such careers out of the social-science enterprise, as if it were unprofessional to rely on personal skills like writing, to assert political and moral values, to direct one's work to public readerships, and to accept "lay" evaluation of the words one produces. But professionalism is not the be-all of life. What is good for the established disciplines is not necessarily good for social science as a whole, nor for the larger society to which it belongs, nor yet for the individual social scientist, whose purpose remains the provision of helpful words to the larger society. This latter purpose, service to the outside community, must be in the life of each one of us the overriding, determining standard of what to say and write and of how to make a living while doing so.

The large, fragmented university remains, of course, the chief context available for a social-science career. Even here, the boundaries between established professions can be crossed. One common way is by creating interdisciplinary programs, centres and institutes. Their usual object is to draw members of competing professions together on the basis of common interest in and knowledge of some topic of current interest–perhaps a country or region, more often a public issue like women's rights, the social impact of technology, or problems of the aged. But these interdisciplinary ventures vary greatly in their usefulness for vitalizing scholarship. Some are mere facades erected in response to the availability of research funds on whatever topic–temporary conspiracies of academic opportunists in disparate fields. Others are places where professors disinclined to systematic and abstract thought can gather to exchange information about a favorite topic–substitutes for intellectual discipline rather than embodiments of it. Still others achieve coherence and vitality, only to grow eventually into new professions, with their own self-serving journals, learned societies, and claims on jobs–thereby increasing overspecialization instead of reducing it.

If you plan to work in a giant university, the hope for your career lies less in interdisciplinary centres or institutes than in your own self. For once you are tenured, the freedom guaranteed to you is enormous–so wide that, as is well known, many professors retain their jobs while producing only worthless words for students and no words at all for anybody else. But what is abused can also be put to good use. Academic freedom means that, regardless of your professional identity, regardless of what department or school you are in, you can scrounge about and follow your nose to ideas your students and readers are desperate to know. You can practice your own discipline, develop and extend it, whether it happens to fall within one of the established disciplines or not. The freedom of tenure allows you to become not just an economist, geographer, or psychologist but a social scientist in your own right–or still more broadly, a scholar ready to cross any boundary without guilt or apology for the sake of producing the exact words people in our time need to hear and read.[15] Tenure allows you as well to cultivate reciprocal relationships with other scholars of whatever stripe, and with students and others in the nonacademic world–relationships that will keep you from becoming an isolate, maverick or crank, however often you may be considered such by colleagues wrapped up in professional affairs.

Social science cannot help but be divided into disciplines. No one could learn all the ideas that go by this name in our time, much less believe them all at once. If your work is to have worth, it will have to form part of some tradition of social scientific scholarship, some more or less orderly set of premises, concepts, theories, and so on.[16] You personally will have to be part of an ongoing intellectual community, one that extends from classical, seminal thinkers long dead through your own generation to the students who will inherit it all and work it over as they see fit. The point here is just not to confuse the discipline you practice with the professional label you happen to wear. What counts is not how good a sociologist you are, social worker, anthropologist, political scientist, or whatever, but how good a servant you are, through the words you produce, of the people who produce more than words–like the food you eat and clothes you wear.

Three Cardinal Principles

How can a social scientist know if the words he or she produces are useful or not? There is no way of knowing for sure. Sticking to the facts is not enough. The facts to which you stick may be beside the point, or on the brink of becoming nonfacts. Popularity is not the answer either, despite current reliance on criteria like book sales, student approval ratings, and audience applause. If no one listens to or reads your words, you clearly fail. But if lots of people gobble your words up appreciatively, you may simply be amusing them, confirming their prejudices, or pandering to their baser sides. What if other people act on the basis of your ideas, implement them in new social programs and institutions? Does this guarantee success? Of course not. The application of your words may turn out to have disastrous consequences.

There is nothing to do but admit the uncertainty of human life, an uncertainty from which word producers are no more exempt than producers of anything else. Scholarship is sometimes sought as an escape from the vagaries and vicissitudes of action. But there is no escape. The beginning of wisdom is surrender to this fact, acceptance that no argument is ever clinched, acknowledgement that there are no definitive data, no confirmed hypotheses, no conclusive evidence. If you live in the consciousness of this truth, you are more likely to think of the right words for your moment in time and space. In Chapter 3 herein, Lasch argues that the public philosophy we need must "rest on an acknowledgement of our dependent position in the world, of the limits of human knowledge, and of our need for others who nevertheless remain separate from ourselves. It is the discovery of human limits that creates the possibility of fraternity."[17]

Beyond a confession of contingency, which words are the right ones depends first of all on who you are and what substantive knowledge you possess. It depends also on who your listeners are and what problems worry them. On both these counts there are obviously huge differences among readers of this book. Hence you must each to some degree work out your own principles for doing social science well. Nonetheless, three basic principles are quite generally relevant. Around them the chapters of this book are arranged. They deserve to be formulated briefly here in turn.

Acceptance of human agency

Everyone is born a bigot. Every human being begins life in a particular social situation which, for lack of broader experience, is accepted as a natural reality, as a matter not of choice or invention but simply of fact. The child cannot possibly know that the relationships into which he or she is born are structured in just one of the millions of ways so far attempted on this earth. The child knows only that these specific relationships—first the family, later the neighbourhood and school, still later the national society—make in his or her case the difference between hunger and satisfaction, rejection and acceptance, ultimately death and life. Thus does the child identify wholeheartedly, even dogmatically, with the relationships at hand. Witness how a preschooler grips a parent's hand when faced with some new experience.

To grow as a person is to broaden one's experience of the social bond, to enter into relationships of many different kinds, to encounter steadily more of the human variety, so that an awareness begins to dawn that life is after all a process of choice, invention, contention, negotiation and debate, that collectively we human beings do make our world. This awareness goes by many names: modernity, autonomy, broadmindedness, maturity, a sense of history.[18] Often this awareness is described by reference to the intellectual movements of the past that nourished it: humanism in the fourteenth to sixteenth centuries, the Reformation, the eighteenth-century Enlightenment or Age of Reason, the French Revolution, nineteenth-century evolutionary theory, the Catholic aggiornamento, and continuing belief in the possibility of progress. But for understanding these diverse historical awakenings to the social fact, nothing serves so well as reflection on one's own biography. Probably you can recall the relationships that opened your eyes to the socially constructed character of earthly life—moments when, like a child first learning to walk, you rose at once terrified and overjoyed to a dizzying height above the social order you once took as absolute. You know also that an historical consciousness is not a once-and-for-all achievement but a process that continues each time some previously unnoticed assumption gives way to knowledge of alternatives.

The first principle on the present list for doing social science well is to be more grown up than most people have the chance to be. Most people's work ties them closely to particular immediate realities. Your work with words allows you to observe the realities of other places, other times. Your job is thus to introduce readers and listeners to new alternatives, to acquaint them with the pros and cons of diverse kinds of relationship, to reduce the taken-for-grantedness in their lives and to increase the intentionality and purpose. Why else should you be paid? Are you worth your salt if you reinforce the entrapment of your audience in its present reality, if you use your words to shield others from awareness that people are in charge and that options exist? Clearly not, even if the powers that be pay you well for doing so, in order to preserve their own privilege. The human species is already hobbled by material exigencies and by habits that are hard to break. Your words are not needed as a further handicap. If you ever describe some way of life as "the way things have to be," you fail. For the reality of human life, whose student you are by occupation privileged to be, is otherwise.

Appropriately, the first of the chapters of this book is Kenneth Gergen's statement of the socially constructed character of social life, including even the words of social scientists. This chapter invites you to grow up in the truest and hardest sense, namely to acknowledge that even the findings of your research are a matter of human agency, a product of human relationships. Gergen writes with an understandable sense of elation at this acknowledgement. Many social scientists of the past, many even today, have thought themselves exempt from history, imagined that even if governmental laws are matters of choice and invention, their own social scientific laws are matters of fact. Such is the positivist philosophy to which generations of scholars have clung dogmatically. Gergen cites some of the authors who have raised our community to a greater height of maturity: Ludwig Wittgenstein, Thomas S. Kuhn, Richard Rorty, P. K. Feyerabend, among others. He draws their insights, moreover, to a practical conclusion for judging a theory's worth: not its accuracy but its "generativity," the extent to which it "departs from the accepted conventions of intelligibility, and in so doing throws reality into question and opens new potentials for action and growth." In so far as you come up with generative theories for the audiences facing you, you will succeed in your job.

One obvious implication of Gergen's argument, as of any acknowledgement of human agency, is the need to study history. If our world has no other knowable origin except relationships between people and between them and the earth, then the way to understand our world is to trace these relationships through time. And if part of our world is an aware, enlightened social science, then we must ask from whence it comes. Chapter 2 herein, David MacGregor's exposition and application of Hegel's thought, gives an important part of the answer. Hegel's position in the history of social science is singular.[19] No earlier thinker, not ibn-Khaldun in the fourteenth century nor Giambattista Vico or Immanuel Kant in the eighteenth, is a match for Hegel in consciousness of human agency. Virtually all later proponents of this self-consciousness draw their insight in part from the Jena philosopher: Wilhelm Dilthey, Karl Marx, Karl Mannheim, Benedetto Croce, John Dewey, R. G. Collingwood, Herbert Marcuse, and many, many more. No one has ever claimed that Hegel is easy to read. MacGregor understands and appreciates him as few contemporary scholars do. His essay here is a plea for recognition that thinking, acting men and women are responsible for the shape our world is in–and for whatever is said about it.

Yet like other affirmations of the historical, humanly constructed character of social science, the chapters by Gergen and MacGregor will be for you just so many pages in a book, except in so far as you personally become entangled in the human variety. Only as you broaden your own experience of the social bond, form relationships with people of diverse occupations, classes, nationalities and historical epochs, will your awareness of human agency become authentic, and your acknowledgement of it more than empty words.[20] It is no accident that all the authors represented in this book have allowed themselves to be buffeted by diverse and contradictory experience. Indeed half of them (Tuan, Baum, Gil, Roweis) make their lives in societies markedly different from their childhood homes. None of them, so far as I know, is limited to just one of the scores of languages spoken on this earth. Nor has any of them enclosed himself within the boundaries of a single profession. In the published work of each of them, moreover, steady and extensive reading of history is apparent, and the cultivation of relationships with people of the past. In sum, maturity as a social scientist means more than mouthing the words of the Enlightenment. It means feeling the Enlightenment in your bones and expressing it in your own words, on the basis of your own involvement in conflicting expressions of the social fact.

Moral engagement

The great advantage of a child's mentality is certainty about right and wrong. To the extent that your identity is tied to a narrow range of relationships, conformity and virtue look very much alike, and so do deviance and vice. But to the extent that you enlarge your acquaintance with the human variety and spread your identity across relationships of different kinds, your morality acquires an iffiness or flexibility. You lose your absolutes and come to see that right and wrong are relative to time and place. If you are asked, perhaps after a lecture, what ought to be done about this or that, you find yourself pondering the range of possibilities and answering, "Well, it depends." This is appropriate and good. It is in any case an essential consequence of growing up, reaching maturity as a social scientist.

But a worthy practice of social science requires more than this, more than a review of options available, more than a relativistic stance. The second cardinal principle offered here is to become morally engaged, to

cultivate not just knowledge but wisdom, not only awareness of alternatives but judgment as to which of them is best here and now. All the
authors in this book affirm this principle. Gergen, for instance, admits
that his perspective is relativist but denies that this means that "anything
goes," arguing instead that "constructionism reasserts the relevance of
moral criteria for scientific practice."[21] The difference between Parts
One and Two of this book is therefore not that Gergen and MacGregor
want to continue debating while the next four authors want closure. All
these authors want both, and rightly so. For however aware we become
of the multiple realities people have made on this earth, we live in a
specific reality: the Western world of the late twentieth century. This
reality will not stand still while we map the countless directions in which
it might possibly move. Human life is indeed a process, but one punctu-
ated by decisions at every turn. We live this process, always at a punctua-
tion point–and this is what the chapters by Lasch, Baum, Tuan and
Gagnon emphasize.[22]

You are not urged here to retain certain acquired or inherited absolutes as boundaries on your historical consciousness, much less to use the
platform of social science for expressing them. Some social scientists are
only 90 percent grown up. They admit the evanescent, historically condi-
tioned, socially constructed character of almost all ways of human life,
meanwhile clutching the consoling thought that males are by nature
polygamous, that people are naturally competitive, that Christianity is
the one true religion, or that some other aspect of life is beyond human
responsibility. And so, when asked to become morally engaged, they
answer by hurling their security blankets at the people they are supposed
to serve. This is no service at all. The problems in our world will not be
solved by escape from freedom into any naive faith–whether in God,
country, science, or whatever else. The kind of social scientist we need is
one who comes fully into the daylight of modernity, one who is able, in
Max Weber's memorable if sexist phrase, "to bear the fate of the times
like a man,"[23] and who then takes the risk of moral engagement.

Nor are you urged to become an advocate of some disadvantaged class
or social category–like women, minorities, the Third World, the "poor
and oppressed"–and to conduct your scientific work on its behalf.
Moralism of this kind is popular among left-wing academics, and it
contrasts nicely with the support of the rich and powerful by right-wing
colleagues. But it rests on an unsustainable separation of fact and value,
as if social scientists were alchemists who could decide with whom to
share their secret knowledge of how life really is.[24] In Chapter 3 herein,
Christopher Lasch is explicitly critical of this kind of Enlightenment
scholar, whether of the "insider" or "outsider" variety. In Chapter 4,
Gregory Baum similarly rejects the setting of scientific, technical knowledge on one side, ethics on the other. We social scientists do not stand

outside the brawl of history with a war chest of information and skills that can be lent at our discretion to one or another competing side. We are in the brawl ourselves. We are products of it, beneficiaries of it, participants in it along with everybody else.

The moral engagement requested here is nothing less than your commitment to the social fact of society in our time, hence your formulation and propagation of a reasoned, provisional, open-ended vision of the public good. You are asked to enter into conversation with other societies past and present, not just to become aware of the range of possibilities but to determine which particular possibility we here and now should try to realize. For we are all in this together: intellectuals and people in practical affairs, management and labour, women and men, unemployed youth and retired aged, the child abuser and the abused child, the one who flunks and the one who gets an A. Reality consists not of these and those social categories, but of the connections. In calling for your contribution to a public philosophy, Lasch asks that you use your knowledge of alternatives to help sketch a social fact worthy of contemporary aspirations. If you then speak for the dispossessed, he points out, it will not be to distance yourself from readers and listeners or to proclaim your own moral superiority, but "to awaken the sense of common ties, the ties of humanity itself, that link the lowest and highest and thereby chasten the pride of wealth and rank." For guidance in the construction of a public philosophy, Lasch cites two exemplars, C. Wright Mills and Melanie Klein.

Moral engagement of this kind is hard. There is immense if false security in denial of the social bond, in the pretense that your social scientific words are independent of your relationship with other people. When you claim to "let the facts speak for themselves," you are disguising your own voice, evading the social fact, trying to keep yourself invulnerable. In Chapter 4, Gregory Baum recommends a better option: that you lay your cards on the table, reveal your ethical vision for the society at hand, and defend it with rational arguments.[25] One special virtue of Baum's chapter is that here he exemplifies his own advice. He traces part of his own biography, acknowledging his relationships with Catholicism, with Scheler, Mannheim, Berger, Weber, the Frankfurt School, Troeltsch and Tillich. He lets you see where he is coming from, the better for you to decide which way to go. Understandably you might resist. Are you going to take seriously a scholar who shows his hand? But this is what moral engagement means: playing the game as if it were more than a game, because it is.

An embrace of the social bond in our time is especially hard for those who are privileged to know and ponder the social bond in other times. Why should you take this society seriously when you know that it, too, will pass? On the other hand, why should this society exempt you from material production so that you can pursue such knowledge, if all it gets in return is cynical, disdainful analyses? Yi-Fu Tuan does not resolve this dilemma rationally in Chapter 5. As much as Lasch and Baum, he accepts the limits of reason. But this beautiful essay itself shows the only way this dilemma can satisfactorily be resolved: by what used to be called an act of will, a cry of yes to the process of becoming, a falling in love with the human project, a wild leap of commitment to its unknowable purpose or lack thereof.[26] Nothing but this allows him to propose and discuss an open-ended concept of the public good. For Tuan as for any mature scholar, virtue and conformity cannot be identical. The good person is one who is "capable of transcending the customs when necessary." Moral engagement does not therefore mean sanctimonious adherence to the norms prevailing in today's world. It means joining others in the critical work of deciding which of these norms should be retained and which replaced in tomorrow's world. Tuan endorses the metaphor of game and theater commonly employed by social scientists. But the real world, he adds, is a morality play, fundamentally serious despite the amusement and farce it may contain.

The final chapter of Part Two seems at first only an illustration or application of the combination of historical consciousness and moral engagement the preceding chapters recommend. The author's appreciative citation of Christopher Lasch only confirms this impression. By systematic critique of research on one particular topic, Serge Gagnon highlights the danger of picking from the past and celebrating those data which cast our own society in a favourable light, the danger of doing social science in a way that serves not the larger human project but our status quo. Gagnon advocates, here as in his books, a thoroughgoing empirical openness to the data of other societies, a readiness to admit the pluralism of human realities. But this is not to evade ethical concern for our own circumstance, instead to make this concern better informed and more reasonable. As he remarks at the start, "The *how* of the science of history can never eliminate the crucial question of *why*." To this latter question Gagnon here spells out an answer, referring specifically to one subject of inquiry.

This subject, however, is sex, and therein lies the chapter's special worth. The moral engagement called for in this book extends, to be sure, far beyond sexual conduct. Yet as Tuan points out in his chapter, the word *moral* is most commonly used in this narrower sense. This is not a linguistic accident. For the sexually active and the celibate alike, sex is the quintessential context for choosing whether to embrace the social bond or not, admit dependency or not, fall in love or not, take life seriously or be cynical. No other aspect of life signals so vividly the essential, defining fact of relationship. Maybe this is why information about sex and reproduction is popularly called the facts of life. When

Gagnon demands that freedom and responsibility be joined, he argues in effect that the development of the self, the personal acquisition of intellectual and physical autonomy, has no purpose except to enter more fully, more constructively, more joyfully into reciprocal relationships with others. If the course of change in a society leaves individuals richer and smarter but more enclosed within themselves, if it leaves them masturbating in solitude or screwing one another for their respective private purposes, then humanity itself is being lost. Such is the basis of Gagnon's doubt about the sexual revolution of our day.

Having read the four chapters in Part Two, you will understand more clearly why an historical consciousness does not imply that "anything goes." The one thing that cannot go up for grabs is the social fact, the common bond of humans with each other, however varied its manifestations across space and time. Nature apart, this bond is all that ever stands between the end of our species and a new beginning. To engage yourself morally in the historical process at hand, to develop a provisional concept of the public good and to take the risk of offering it toward a public philosophy–this to accept the social fact. To remain aloof and superior, to make "It depends" the only response of your intellectual career–this is to deny the relationship that your existence demonstrates you have. It would be truly antisocial behaviour. It might even be described–only you can know–by the word we social scientists fanatically avoid: evil.[27]

Practicality

The three principles around which this book is organized are arranged in descending order of distance from the society immediately confronting you. First you are asked to take flight from this society and to explore all kinds of alternatives, gaining thereby a consciousness of history and human agency. The second principle asks that you nonetheless embrace this society, become morally engaged to it, and join in formulating a vision of some better alternative toward which it might move. Now finally you are urged to help make this movement happen, by involving yourself in the nuts and bolts of social change. Between the *is* of today's way of life and the *ought* of a public philosophy stands an intimidating range of tasks: public education, publicity, securing funds, building a communications network, mobilizing support, taking over existing organizations, building new ones, co-opting or defeating still other ones, fighting in courtrooms and the streets, rearranging the structures of power and wealth, replacing elites, reorganizing production, and so on and on. If the conception of the good life you come to espouse is to be more than a pie in the sky, you must attend–as a social scientist–to the procedures necessary for moving history toward it. Your job is not only to come up with something worthwhile to say but to say it to such an audience on such an occasion in such a way that it will have the practical effect of changing for the better the way people relate to one another.

Avoidance of practical concerns is an occupational hazard for any word producer, even one who is morally engaged. Making words fit with one another is by itself hard work. Ensuring that they also fit with empirical realities is harder work. Conveying through your words in addition a sense of history and a vision of some greater good makes the work still harder. It may seem too much to insist, on top of all this, that your words should also point readers and listeners toward workable strategies of progressive change. This is so especially because taking the final step will get you into trouble with powerful opponents of change who might otherwise applaud your "interesting, inspiring, and insightful" words.[28] But nothing less will do. Unless you indicate some of the steps by which to get from here to there, those who receive your words will treat "there" as a noble fantasy and resign themselves to staying "here." Unless you offer practical guidelines for transformative action, you will remain, despite your good intentions, a servant of the status quo in its battle of inertia against a little better world.

You can be practical at various levels of abstraction. At the conference where the chapters in this book were read, the point was often made that theory is a form of practice. Indeed it is, provided it grabs those who hear or read it so compellingly that they think and act differently thereafter, and in a way that corresponds to what the theory implies. The extent to which theory is a form of practice, this is to say, is a function not of theory but of the human relationship wherein a specific theory is presented and taken in. As a general rule, the more abstract your words are, the more likely their practical implications will go right by your audience or readership. On the other hand, the more concrete your words are, the more they take the form of a recipe, the less likely they are to work. In this as in other respects, success as a social scientist requires keeping your head in the clouds and your feet on the ground at once. It means searching day by day for the words that will hit home, and never quite finding them.[29]

The best measure of the practicality of your words is how much effect they have on the immediate relationships of which you are part. No one knows so well as you the theory of society, history and the public good you are developing. Has it made any difference in the way you behave toward parents and siblings, spouse and children, neighbours, colleagues, friends, students, editors, superiors at work, and the various fellow citizens you encounter in daily life? Has it led you out of some relationships and into others, in a biographical course you consider good? To the extent that you personally have stayed the same in the course of gaining social scientific knowledge, the transformative power of your knowledge is very much in doubt. By contrast, in so far as you have been able, in various small ways, to enhance the quality of your own relationships in light of what you know, your knowledge has begun to satisfy this third principle of doing social science well. Humbling though it is to admit, you yourself are the best piece of evidence for whether your social science is good for anything.

Beyond their effect on your own life, the best way to assess the practical value of your words is by the response you get from those who receive them. Whoever is given useful words feels an impulse to say thanks, and to inform the giver of the words' effect. Occasionally at least, people act on this impulse even without prompting. Hence as a word producer, you can expect that listeners or readers will from time to time tell you if your words have made any difference in anything. If nothing comes back to you at all, assume the worst. Find new words, new outlets for them, new audiences, a new job, or if all else fails, a new line of work. But if expressions of gratitude pour in unsolicited, do not too quickly take delight in this. Sustained applause, high teaching scores, and fat royalty cheques can mean many different things. Instead read and listen to what your admirers actually report. Find out precisely which human relationships, if any, changed on account of your words, and whether the change was in the direction you intended or (as often happens) contrary to it. It is the change in life as it is lived, not the esteem in which you are held, that tells the place you have, as a social scientist, in history.

The two final chapters in this book share with those preceding both acknowledgement of human agency and moral engagement in the human project. They are placed in the separate, concluding section only because of their emphasis on practicality, the pointedness of their demand that knowledge serve everyday people in their everyday lives—"at the street level," as Shoukry Roweis put it at the conference. It happens also that he and David Gil, in their respective presentations, excelled all the other speakers in the passion and personal witness apparent in their words. This is saying quite a lot, since nearly all the presentations were powerful. One participant wrote afterwards that Gil was "something else." "There was something about *how* he confronts his questions that I thought exemplary. In a sense he went beyond argument. He was speaking about experience." Another described Gil's address as "a fine balance of lucid reasoning and deep, unrelenting commitment to the human race and what it could be."[30]

Roweis differed from Gil on many counts, as a comparison of their chapters herein will show you, but the response to his address was no less intense. Many of the more cerebral, academic participants were outraged at his apparent desecration of their work. "Roweis is an apologist for terrorism," one muttered afterwards. In the question period Gil disputed some point of history. Roweis bristled in response, as if shrinking from the mire of intellectual debate. On the level of theory, Roweis's chapter here is probably best compared with Gergen's. Despite their different intellectual approaches, social constructionism versus the work of Foucault, they share a supreme openness to the human variety. But in the priority on practical knowledge, Roweis shares more with Gil. Their papers belong together here. Their farewell embrace at the end of the conference spoke more than words.

Conclusion

Before you begin reading the chapters of this book, you should be fore-warned that they do not constitute a codified, unified, utterly consistent body of thought about how to practice social science well. There is a fair amount of unity, of course, as this introduction has made clear. But these chapters will not engross you as a novel might, or dazzle you with a poem's symmetry. This is not their purpose, nor that of any social scientific work. Tuan notes in his chapter a contemporary tendency to glorify coherence and unity in the words of social scientists, whether they are relevant to the real, external world or not.[31] MacGregor cites an example of this tendency, the fact that most articles in the leading economics journal have no data at all, just elegant mathematical models. But to make inherent, intrinsic qualities the chief expectation for our articles and books is to detach social science from the flux of life. This book neither encourages such detachment nor caters to it. It is meant not to be enjoyed as if it were a work of abstract art, but to be studied, criticized, turned over in your mind, reflected on in light of your own experience, and taken to heart for its practical value in your own work and life.

If you imagine this book as a musical performance, do not expect a classical symphony or single composition but a series of eight authentic folk songs about how to write folk music for our time. This introduction has highlighted common themes, pulled the performance together more or less, but the songs remain separate. If you try to just sit back and enjoy, you won't. The only way to get anything out of this book is to approach it actively as an involved member of the human community at issue, one whose special work is to produce for people here and now words that will serve them well. The performers in this book have put themselves on the line. If you are to appreciate their words, you have to do the same. You need not like them all. Perhaps only three or four say things precisely relevant to the work you want to do. Not to worry. The songs are short, sincere, and to the point, and the singers have made it in their own careers. Just let go, listen closely, and keep looking for ideas you can use.

If, in the midst of the diversity herein, you are able to see the underlying commonality of outlook, and if you find this outlook generally sound and sensible, you may find yourself wanting a name for it. There is some danger in this. Numerous labels already define and limit you at work: intellectual, social scientist, member of your particular profession, specialist in some subfield, professor or researcher, and adherent of some theoretical tradition—feminism, functionalism, behaviourism, revisionism, symbolic interactionism, Marxism, Freudianism, liberalism, neoconservatism, or whatever. A further label may do more harm than good. One or two pigeonholes are useful as doorways into public life, but lots of successive pigeonholes within pigeonholes will leave you trapped, stifled, precisely identified and cut off from almost everybody else. If a label must be applied to the kind of social science this book represents, it had best be the broad, inclusive label of *humanism*. By this word is meant simply awareness of the human project, engagement to it, and practical involvement toward moving it along.

All the authors in this book have been called humanists, and with few or many qualms they have accepted this name for themselves. The conference where these chapters were read was the inaugural event of a centre for so-called humanist social science planned for the Waterloo universities. Most of the participants were and remain members of one or more of the perhaps twenty scholarly organizations in North America formally called by the humanist name—groups like the Division of Humanistic Psychology of the American Psychological Association or the Association for Humanist Sociology.[32] The fact remains, moreover, that many social scientists whose work exemplifies in varying ways the principles proposed herein have found the word *humanist* congenial. To cite just a few varied names: William James, John Dewey, Abraham Maslow, Carl Rogers, Erich Fromm, John Kenneth Galbraith, Charles Hampden-Turner, Colin Turnbull, Ashley Montagu, Floyd Matson, Alfred McClung Lee, Peter Berger, Richard Titmuss, Herbert Marcuse, and T. B. Bottomore.

But even so simple and unassailable a name as this has liabilities. In some contexts, notably the American Humanist Association, it connotes an excessive rationalism or scientism, and a thoroughgoing rejection of religion, mystery, the acknowledgement of ultimate dependency.[33] But every single one of the chapters herein displays a keen sense of the limits of knowledge. They signal not a cool, cerebral, detached, controlling social science but one informed by the same mix of hot and cold, body and mind, passion and disinterest, control and surrender, as marks the human condition itself.

A further liability is the undisciplined, namby-pamby colouring the word *humanism* has taken on in many social scientific circles.[34] Humanists are said to be on the soft side of an alleged debate between qualitative and quantitative methods of research, perhaps for lack of mathematical aptitude or of the courage to face up to tough realities. It is true enough that computer expertise is not offered here as a basic principle of social science. But this reflects not any disparagement of technical, statistical, quantitative research skills, but only a wise ordering of priorities. The record shows that Yi-Fu Tuan once held a postdoctoral fellowship in statistics, that Gregory Baum earned a master's degree in mathematics, that Serge Gagnon is associated with an empiricist movement among Quebec historians, and that all the authors in this book rank well above average in ability to be hard-nosed.

Probably the worst thing about identifying as humanist the social scientific principles offered here is that you, the reader, might thereby be invited to pigeonhole yourself more than you already are. Further division might be encouraged, moreover, in a scholarly enterprise already too much divided, too preoccupied with its divisions, and too little in touch with people's everyday lives. The last thing the authors of this book want is to create a sect of humanist social scientists engaged in self-righteous debate about their humanism, while the human project languishes.[35] What we want is that you and all of us earn our salt and produce useful words for the human community that sustains us. It is to help you work out your own way of doing so that this book has been published. Call it humanist social science if you like, but then get on with your important work.[36]

Let me end on a note of regret—one of the few regrets I have in connection with these eight chapters. It happens that men wrote all of them. This was not the original plan. It turned out that of the women invited to give papers at the conference, only one was able to accept. Her paper, moreover, like several others by men, lay outside the scope of this book and hence will be published elsewhere. The absence of women contributors is regrettable not just because a chance to recognize and promote sexual equality is thereby lost but also because so many women exemplify the kind of scholarship this book recommends. One thinks of Hannah Arendt, Ruth Benedict, Joan Robinson, Alva Myrdal, Betty Friedan, Elise Boulding, Jane Jacobs, Barbara Ehrlichman, and many others. This book might almost be directed especially to social scientists of the male sex, since they seem disproportionately in need of its emphases. Still, what matters in a social scientific work is not whether its author is man or woman, but whether it cultivates the common life men and women share.

NOTES

1. About twenty commentaries on and reactions to the conference were published in the fall of 1986 in a tabloid entitled *The Conference in Retrospect*, which was distributed to conference participants from my office at the University of Waterloo. Citations to this publication in later footnotes identify it by title only.
2. Chicago: University of Chicago Press, 1938, first published 1938. For a recent critique of Durkheim's influence and a compelling invitation to transcend his conception of social science, see Stanley R. Barrett, *The Rebirth of Anthropological Theory* (Toronto: University of Toronto Press, 1984).
3. Ashley Montagu has made the quote from Donne almost the trademark of his own writing. See especially his *On Being Human* (New York: Hawthorn, 1966). Three other classic statements of the essentially social character of human existence are Martin Buber, *Between Man and Man* (Boston: Beacon, 1955), Norbert Elias, "Introduction to the 1968 Edition," pp. 219-63 of his *The History of Manners* (New York: Pantheon, 1978; first published 1939), and Karl Mannheim, *Ideology and Utopia* (New York: Harcourt, Brace and World, 1936). In the latter Mannheim writes, "Strictly speaking it is incorrect to say that the single individual thinks. Rather it is more correct to insist that he participates in thinking further what other men have thought before him" (p. 3).
4. The term *social bond* is herein taken as a synonym for *social fact*; the reference is to Werner Stark's rich, four-volume treatise under this title (New York: Fordham University Press, 1977-1983). The problem of how to serve the common good while at the same time allowing individual self-assertion has preoccupied a long lineage of scholars, from Hobbes to Tocqueville on to our own day. For a contemporary example see Robert N. Bellah *et al.*, *Habits of the Heart* (Berkeley: University of California Press, 1985), the best part of which is its appendix on "Social Science as Public Philosophy." The key point is that the quest for selfhood is in vain except in the context of powerful, reciprocal relationships. For discussion of current vanity in this respect, see Christopher Lasch, *The Culture of Narcissism* and *The Minimal Self* (New York: Norton, 1979 and 1984 respectively), as well as the earlier classic by David Riesman, *The Lonely Crowd* (New Haven: Yale University Press, 1950).
5. One excellent overview of the contemporary world of work, a depiction that puts in relief the privileged positions of social scientists, is James W. Rinehart, *The Tyranny of Work* (Toronto: Harcourt Brace Jovanovich Canada, 1987).
6. The radical difference between studying nature and studying people is a recurrent theme in modern social science. One especially lucid recent statement is Charles Taylor, *Social Theory as Practice* (Delhi: Oxford University Press, 1983). But to bolster the point further, I should also cite two splendid books by non-social scientists: *Computer Power and Human Reason* (New York: Penguin, 1976, 1984) by computer scientist Joseph Weizenbaum, and *The Mismeasure of Man* (New York: Norton, 1981), by biologist Stephen Jay Gould. To distinguish between people and nature by no means implies "that whatever is other than man is an object to be used, a utility" (Lawrence Haworth, *Decadence and Objectivity*, Toronto: University of Toronto Press, 1977, p. 107). Haworth rightly rejects this attitude but wrongly calls it humanism. Recognition of human uniqueness does not rule out a respectful, reciprocal relationship with nature, nor with what lies beyond both nature and humanity. See Caroline Richards, "On Subduing the Earth: the Suzuki Critique," *Grail* 1 (December 1985), pp. 95-100.
7. Yi-Fu Tuan makes and extends this point in his chapter in this book. This is not, of course, to deny how much social scientists share with many producers of literary words. Michael Higgins made this point well in his critical comment on the conference from which this book derives (*The Conference in Retrospect*, p. 4). He would like, he wrote, at least to have heard references to scholars like Matthew Arnold, John Ruskin, or Northrop Frye.
8. Serge Gagnon, *Man and His Past* (Montreal: Harvest House, 1982), p. vii. This book is an excellent introduction not only to historiography but to the social scientific enterprise itself.

9. The solution to this problem is by no means simply to transfer our allegiance to the downtrodden, as Howard Becker seemed to suggest in 1966, in his presidential address to the Society for the Study of Social Problems, entitled "Whose Side Are We On?" Alvin Gouldner published a spirited critique of Becker's proposal, more worth reading now than it was then, which ended with this memorable sentence: "It is to values, not to factions, that sociologists must give their most basic commitment." Both papers, along with others equally of interest, are reprinted in Jack D. Douglas, ed., *The Relevance of Sociology* (New York: Appleton-Century-Crofts, 1970). See also Gouldner's *Coming Crisis of Western Sociology* (New York: Avon, 1970). Needless to say, both these books apply to social science in general, not just to the profession named in their titles.

10. It behooves every social scientist teaching in a college or university to study at length the actual purposes these institutions serve in their graduates' lives. The place to start is the last chapter of Thorstein Veblen's *Theory of the Leisure Class* (New York: New American Library, 1953; first published 1899), and his book, *The Higher Learning in America* (New York: Sagamore, 1957; first published 1918). I recommend also the chapters on education in A. F. Laidlaw, ed., *The Man from Margaree: Writings and Speeches of M. M. Coady* (Don Mills, Ont.: McClelland and Stewart, 1971), and of course, Paolo Freire, *Pedagogy of the Oppressed* (New York: Seabury, 1970). My modest contribution to the ample literature in this regard is entitled "Becoming Rootless by Degrees," *Past and Present* (1986).

11. One-dimensional empiricism ties a social scientist's tongue on policy issues, so that any normative statements come out disguised, garbled, twisted around. One recent example is the policy statement, *On the Treatment of the Sexes in Research*, promulgated by the Social Sciences and Humanities Research Council of Canada (Ottawa: SSHRCC, 1985). Written by Margrit Eichler and Jeanne Lapointe, the statement rests on the laudable value of improving the condition of Canadian women. But it does not put this value up front, assert it openly, defend it systematically, and then draw implications for the conduct of research. Instead the pamphlet is couched in terms of "excellence in research," the elimination of "biases which distort reality," the need to "correct errors and false interpretations," and adherence to "standards of scientific objectivity." The authors seem oblivious to the fact that if our ancestors had shaped their minds and words to fit the "reality" then in place, women would today be a great deal worse off than they are—and so would men. It is only because our ancestors mixed realism and idealism, produced words congruent with both existing realities and higher ideals, that some measure of progressive change has indeed occurred. Goethe wrote that "if we take our fellow-men as they are, we make them worse than they are" (quoted in Stark, *The Social Bond*, Vol. 4, p. 128). I am confident he meant to include women in his sentiment. For a splendid practical guide to policy research, see Howard Richards, *The Evaluation of Cultural Action* (New York: Humanities, 1985).

12. As their respective introductions make clear, this was the main procedure for defining the scope of both the *Encyclopedia of the Social Sciences* (New York: Macmillan, 1930-35) and the *International Encyclopedia of the Social Sciences* (New York: Macmillan, 1968).

13. For developing a critical understanding of what professions are about, Ivan Illich's books are an excellent place to start: *Deschooling Society* (New York: Harper and Row, 1970), *Toward a History of Needs* (New York: Pantheon, 1977), and especially the co-authored *Disabling Professions* (Don Mills, Ont.: Burns and MacEachern, 1977).

14. Such portrayal is part of the ideology of professionalization. See Everett C. Hughes, "Higher Education and the Professions," in C. Kaysen, ed., *Content and Context: Essays on College Education* (New York: McGraw-Hill, 1973).

15. This is a paraphrase of Everett Hughes in his article, "The Improper Study of Man," pp. 20-28 in W. R. Scott, ed., *Social Processes and Social Structures* (New York: Holt, Rinehart and Winston, 1970). Hughes himself rose above the boundaries of established disciplines, as have most of the great social scientists, from Karl Marx to E. F. Schumacher.

16. The refusal to make your work part of a tradition serves vanity at the cost of effectiveness. See Christopher Lasch, *Haven in a Heartless World* (New York: Basic Books, 1979), p. 51.

17. I count this the most important insight in this whole book, and Lasch is not by any means the only one who offers it. Jan Smith, for instance, has applauded the tradition Gergen's chapter represents on grounds that "it warns against pride, against a presumption of, even a hankering for, omniscience" (*Conference in Retrospect*, p. 2). Although neither Lasch nor Gergen identifies the acknowledgement of limits and dependency as a religious attitude, I have gone so far as to define religion in precisely these terms–see my *First Sociology* (New York: McGraw-Hill, 1982). This may help explain why a scholar like Gagnon, whose humility takes more explicitly religious expression, is nonetheless so much in tune with Lasch.

18. This is not the place to argue for any particular expression of historical consciousness or any specific strand of modern thought. The point is rather to contrast mature, processual thinking with immature, close-minded, static mentalities–as represented by ancient and medieval philosophy, positive science, and what Max Weber identified as traditionalism in peasant societies. Let me offer a broad range of references: Ernst Cassirer, *The Philosophy of the Enlightenment* (Boston: Beacon, 1960); H. Stuart Hughes, *Consciousness and Society: the Reorientation of European Social Thought, 1890-1930* (New York: Knopf, 1958); Franklin Baumer, *Modern European Thought* (New York: Macmillan, 1977); Crane Brinton, "Enlightenment," in the *Encyclopedia of Philosophy* (New York: Macmillan, 1967); Henri Bergson, *Creative Evolution* (New York: Random House, 1944); Erich Fromm, *Escape from Freedom* (New York: Rinehart, 1941); Rollo May, *Freedom and Destiny* (New York: Delta, 1981); John Passmore, *The Perfectibility of Man* (London: Duckworth, 1970); Ernest Becker, *The Denial of Death* (New York: Free Press, 1973); and Peter Berger *et al.*, *The Homeless Mind* (New York: Random House, 1973). Here at least, I am less keen on promoting one or another of these authors than on encouraging all social scientists to become familiar with this literature and to draw their respective conclusions as free women and men.

19. On Hegel's significance in the history of social thought, see Herbert Marcuse, *Reason and Revolution* (New York: Humanities, 1963), and Charles Taylor, *Hegel and Modern Society* (Cambridge: Cambridge University Press, 1979). In my keynote address to the Association for Humanist Sociology in 1983, I traced to Hegel four important traditions of humanist social science: Marxism, the sociology of knowledge, the Frankfurt School, and American pragmatism.

20. This amounts to a recommendation that you make and keep yourself "marginal"–in the sense that Robert Park used the term in his introduction to E. V. Stonequist, *The Marginal Man* (New York: Scribner's, 1937). It is advice to remain something of a "stranger" in the society at hand–see Georg Simmel, "The Sociological Significance of the 'Stranger,'" pp. 322-27 in R. E. Park and E. W. Burgess, eds., *Introduction to the Science of Sociology* (Chicago: Univ. of Chicago Press, 1924). For one striking illustration of this point, see Paul Tillich, *On the Boundary: an Autobiographical Sketch* (New York: Charles Scribner's Sons, 1966). A brief quote from the last-named (p. 97): "The man who stands on many boundaries experiences the unrest, insecurity, and inner limitation of existence in many forms."

21. "The Social Constructionist Movement in Modern Psychology," *American Psychologist* 40 (March 1985), p. 273.

22. A further paper from the conference not included here, the only presentation not made by an academic, also emphasized moral engagement. Robert Bandeen, former head of Canadian National Railways, highlighted the importance of reflecting on and setting goals–especially when this is most difficult, namely in a time of rapid change. Goal-setting implies a certain resignation to the necessity of acting in the reality at hand, even if this is just one of a million possible realities. The formulation of goals for the human community in general, and the immediate one in particular, is an integral part of building a public philosophy.

23. "Science as a Vocation," in H. H. Gerth and C. W. Mills, *From Max Weber* (New York: Oxford, 1946), p. 155.

24. Miguel de Unamuno once referred to sociologists as "the astrologers and alchemists of our twentieth century." This was not because Unamuno thought sociology as then propagated was empirically inaccurate, but because it was presented as if independent of human relationships.

25. The analogy limps, since in a card game you can assume that each player knows his or her own hand. Knowledge of real life is harder to come by. Psychologist David Bakan, in a gripping conference presentation not included in this book, spoke of "secrets, the repressing of what we know, the not-knowing of what we know" (see S. K. Johannesen, *The Conference in Retrospect*, p. 2). It is only by sincere, hard reflection on yourself that you find out which cards you hold, that is, become aware of the relationships that limit you, tie you down, and define who you are. Only as you gain such self-awareness can you communicate it to others and thus make your social scientific words liberating rather than manipulative. This, I think, is what Yi-Fu Tuan means when he says, "In a future conference, perhaps we can make it a rule that scholars have to speak in their own voices" (*Conference in Retrospect*, p. 2).

26. The phrase, of course, is Kierkegaard's. I would not argue, however, that this leap is altogether independent of social context. On the contrary, personal involvement in dynamic, constructive, reciprocal relationships makes an embrace of the social bond much easier, even for one who knows that all relationships are transient. In an unpublished paper, "Living with an Historical Consciousness" (1984), I made the point as best I could: "People don't need to feel they've arrived, so long as they seem to be headed together toward something worthy of their time." This is itself a paraphrase of one of J. R. Smallwood's best lines: "It's not where you are that counts; it's where you're headed."

27. I do not see how it is possible to develop a concept of goodness without also developing, at least by implication, a concept of evil. I would argue that repudiation of dependence on what is outside oneself is at least the beginning of what evil means. But the word should not be thrown around. I am not sure it can ever be applied with confidence to anyone but oneself, since one can never know what strange drummer another might be loving and listening to. Clearly, the condemnation of existing evil is a cheap substitute for the hard work of offering some vision of a greater good.

28. Stepping into practicality also invites contempt and disdain from those utopian intellectuals who cannot admire any concrete plan of action unless in a foreign country or in the distant past. Three speakers at the conference from which this book derives displayed such practicality to heroic degree: Douglas House, recounting his work as head of Newfoundland's royal commission on unemployment; Eleonora Cebotarev, describing her program of action research for and with families in Latin America; and David Ley, who offered the False Creek development in Vancouver as an exemplar of humane urban design. All three of these speakers met with disdain from part of the audience, but this is by no means the reason why their papers are not included here. The reasons are less principled and more mundane. Due to his practical commitments, House did not have his presentation written out. The greater part of Cebotarev's paper got lost in the word processor while she was traveling in Colombia. Ley's very polished paper deserved the graphic illustration he accomplished with slides at the conference, but the budget for this book has not allowed for such. Besides, the inclusion of papers on more particular topics would have tested too much the demand that this book be short, coherent (see footnote 31), and of general appeal to social scientists. But let me confess my deep appreciation of each of these three scholars, and of the practical engagement their work represents.

29. I do not mean to talk in riddles here, but only in a homespun version of dialectical logic. For discussion of the latter see Robert Heilbroner, *Marxism For and Against* (New York: Norton, 1980), J. F. Rychlak, ed., *Dialectic: Humanistic Rationale for Behavior and Development* (Basel, New York: Karger, 1976), several provocative papers on this topic in Kenneth and Mary Gergen, eds., *Historical Social Psychology* (Hillsdale, N.J.: Erlbaum Assoc., 1984), and Damir Mirkovic, *Dialectic and Sociological Thought* (St. Catharine's, Ont.: Diliton, 1980).

30. Comments by Victor Lotter and Malou Twynam in The *Conference in Retrospect*, p. 2 and p. 6 respectively.

31. In his discussion of Gergen's paper (*Conference in Retrospect*, p. 3), J. R. Kelly quoted novelist Peter Dickinson as saying that "the crucial thing for a writer is the ability to make up coherent worlds.... I try to find a voice in my head. I write the books first, then do the research, then rewrite them." Added Kelly, "This is not bad advice, not

merely for aspiring novelists but also for social scientists. I suspect that no graduate student who does not instinctively follow this advice ever completes a thesis." All this is true enough, and I have prudently called Kelly's insight to the attention of graduate students working with me. What makes an acceptable thesis, however, does not precisely coincide with the requirements of useful knowledge.

32. For examples of humanist social science, as the term is actually used, see the following journals, each published by an avowedly humanist professional association: *Anthropology and Humanism Quarterly, Humanist Educator, Humanity and Society,* and *Journal of Humanistic Psychology.* See also the following collections: David Ley and Marvin Samuels, eds., *Humanistic Geography* (Chicago: Maaroufa Press, 1978); Suzanne Mackenzie, ed., *Humanism and Geography* (Ottawa: Carleton University Discussion Paper No. 3, 1986); J. F. Glass and J. R. Staude, eds., *Humanistic Society: Today's Challenge to Sociology* (Pacific Palisades, Calif.: Goodyear, 1972); Richard H. Weller, ed., *Humanistic Education* (Berkeley: McCutchan, 1977); Mortimer J. Adler et al., *Humanistic Education and Western Civilization: Essays for Robert M. Hutchins* (New York: Holt, Rinehart, and Winston, 1964); M. A. Lutz and K. Lox, eds., *The Challenge of Humanistic Economics* (California: Benjamin Cummings, 1979); J. R. Royce and L. P. Mos, eds., *Humanistic Psychology: Concepts and Criticisms* (New York: Plenum, 1981); Frank T. Severin, ed., *Humanistic Viewpoints in Psychology* (New York: McGraw-Hill, 1965); and I. David Welch et al., eds., *Humanistic Psychology: a Sourcebook* (Buffalo: Prometheus, 1978). There are many more social scientific works formally identified as humanist, from Donald R. Hellison's *Humanistic Physical Education* (Englewood Cliffs: Prentice-Hall, 1973), to Norman Pearson's *A Humanist Approach to Land Resources Planning* (Guelph, Ont.: University of Guelph Centre for Resources Development, 1971), to Joseph Levy's "Towards a Humanistic Definition of Play Behavior," *Ontario Psychologist* 13 (January 1981), pp. 10-15.

33. In *The Politics at God's Funeral* (New York: Penguin, 1983), Michael Harrington points out that neither dogmatic atheism nor dogmatic religion is very helpful for resolving the problems of our world. This beautiful book by an exemplar of humanist social science shows the sterility of outdated debates in this respect.

34. Pointedly rejecting this colouring, Glenn Goodwin has stressed the importance of distinguishing between positivism and empiricism, and of retaining the latter while abandoning the former (see *The Conference in Retrospect,* p. 2). See also Jan Loubser et al., "Humanism and Positivism in Sociology and Social Policy," pp. 84-95 in A. W. Rasporich, ed., *The Social Sciences and Public Policy in Canada* (Calgary: University of Calgary Faculty of Social Sciences, 1979).

35. Quite a few commentators in *The Conference in Retrospect* expressed a worry that the cultivation of humanist social science might serve only to insulate social scientists from practical problems. Jon Darling cautioned against an "abstracted humanism...cut off from the lives of people who are not social scientists." Joan Rayfield wrote, "Let us not build yet another ivory tower." Norm Choate reported from his discussion group that in any future conference, "there should be representation from people beyond academia." Doug Lorimer doubted the wisdom of creating a "Centre for Advanced Studies in Humanist Social Science," fearing that "the institutional form may well determine the outcome regardless of whether it practices positivist or humanist social science." On the other hand, practical effectiveness requires that thought be cultivated systematically, and it may even sometimes be helpful to put a name on some body of systematic thought. Richard Preston called wisely for "the establishment of a number of mutual understandings between people whose humanism is developed mainly at a contemplative level, and people whose humanism is expressed mainly in practical action."

36. Rejecting the term *humanistic* for its "ambiguous baggage," John Thompson has suggested instead *human* social sciences (*Conference in Retrospect,* p. 5). But this appelation has baggage of its own, in particular the phenomenological philosophy at the root of Amedeo Giorgi's classic book, *Psychology as a Human Science* (New York: Harper and Row, 1970), and of the several associations and institutes of the "human sciences" now well established. The present book has an affinity for the human-science movement. Several leaders of this movement, Giorgi included, took part in the conference from

which this book derives. But the chapters by both Baum and Roweis herein are explicitly critical of phenomenology. The thrust of this volume is more rational, public, political and practical than phenomenologically inclined social scientists tend to be–whether in the human-science movement or in other currents like interactionism and ethnomethodology. If some label must be applied to the present book, *humanist* remains the more accurate choice, especially given its association with James, Schiller, Dewey, and American pragmatism, with Mannheim and other sociologists of knowledge, and with Fromm, Marcuse, and the Frankfurt School, as also with religious thinkers like Jacques Maritain and Albert Schweitzer.

Part I

ACCEPTANCE OF HUMAN AGENCY

1

ON THE SOCIAL CONSTRUCTION
OF KNOWLEDGE

Kenneth J. Gergen

In recent years many have despaired over the direction and outcomes of social-science inquiry. As it is said, such inquiry has become increasingly technical, specialized and rarefied. As problems of social life become more intense, complex, and life threatening, the sciences have become increasingly remote. Somehow real persons located in historically situated circumstances have fallen through the nomological nets. We now treat only the abstract simulacra of human existence, and in this dispassionate mode of comportment, rob the human venture of deep significance. The call for development of a humanist social science represents one timely reply to such criticisms.

Yet, what are the chances of success for a humanist social science? After all, discontent with the social sciences is hardly novel within the present century. From the twenties through the forties, as the behavioural movement emerged across the spectrum of the social sciences, many voices of anguish could be heard. With the shift toward observables, the rich quality of human experience was being obscured; with the rise of statistical methods, the intricacies of the unique individual were submerged; with the emphasis on systematic determinants, possibilities for human freedom and creativity were denigrated; with the concern for universal principles of behaviour, the view to history was occluded; and with the concern for impartial or objective knowledge, discourse on human values became déclassé. Yet, in spite of such widespread anguish the behavioural movement (or "scientism" in its pejorative form) has continued to flourish. Laboratories, statistical analyses, observational methods, computers, granting agencies, and requisite power structures all have prospered. All have been inspired in large measure by the possibility of making genuine gains in objective knowledge of human behaviour. In many corners of the sciences the word *humanism* is reserved for the antiquated romantic whose tender heartthrobs impede the development of a mature science. Why should we be any more optimistic at the present juncture? Are there emerging developments that favour the emergence of a new and more sophisticated humanism?

I believe the answer to this question is an unqualified affirmative. There are two intellectual waves to be considered, which together both remove the justification for traditional science and furnish a substantial and challenging alternative. The first wave is primarily a critical one, and has largely occurred within the philosophy and history of science. The second wave is more generative in character, and begins to furnish the contours of an alternative metatheory to empiricism–namely that of social construction. Let us consider first the critical wave.

The conception of objective, cumulative knowledge of human behaviour within the social sciences is largely an outgrowth of empiricist theories of knowledge more generally. The promise of the behavioural movement and indeed its chief basis of justification have largely been furnished by logical empiricist philosophy of science. Without a viable conception for science there is no warrant for an empirical science of behaviour. Yet, even in the 1930s there was intense debate within the Vienna Circle over the relationship between observations and scientific propositions. Did each observation correspond to a single word or concept, a "primitive idea," an "atomic proposition," or some other representational implement? The question was never satisfactorily answered. Since this period we have confronted a wide range of stinging arguments against the empiricist view of knowledge. We have confronted arguments against the process of induction (Hanson), the logic of verification (Popper), operationism (Koch), word-object correspondence (Quine), the separation of analytic from synthetic propositions (Quine), the supposed interdependence of theoretical understanding and prediction (Toulmin), the commensurability of competing theories (Feyerabend), the separation of fact and value (MacIntyre), the possibility of theoretically unsaturated or brute facts (Hanson), the logic of deduction (Barrett), the possibility of falsifying theory (Quine), the non-partisan character of scientific knowledge (Habermas), the possibility for the historical accumulation of social knowledge (Gergen), and the applicability of the covering law and mechanistic models to human action (Whyte), to name but a few. In effect, within the philosophy of science there is little left of the optimism of the 1930s. Few remain within philosophy who believe in foundations of incorrigible knowledge–truth through method. Most agree that we are currently in a "post-empiricist" phase–unanchored, at sea, and without apparent rudder. The critical phase has had profound effects outside the behavioural sciences. It is only a matter of time before the repercussions will be felt within the sciences themselves.

As the justification for the empirical foundation of knowledge has deteriorated, new voices have begun to sound. Although retaining the critical spirit they begin to suggest an alternative picture of knowledge–its genesis and evolution. This alternative view is one of broad and dramatic significance for society, and closest attention is invited. To understand this revolution, consider again the story of knowledge as told by the empiricist. At the outset one commences with the assumption of a physical world independent of the knower. The acquisition of knowledge first requires the observer's careful sensitivity to this world (recording the contours of the world as sense data), and the preliminary formulation of hypotheses. These hypotheses then become the basis for logical deductions, which deductions are tested more systematically against new observations. The new observations, in turn, inform the observer of the validity of his or her hypotheses, and enable alterations to be made in such a way that the theory becomes an increasingly precise map of the physical world. Notice here that we have a finely honed narrative in which there is a causal arrow released at the beginning (with the material world), and which, through a series of repercussions (including induction, deduction, test, revision, and so on), ultimately finds its target in the form of an enhanced state of knowledge. It is a story of knowledge that elevates the knowledge maker to commanding status, for it is the maker of knowledge who furnishes the means by which the culture can survive if not thrive. Knowledge is power.

The new voices–disparate in origin and emphasis–provide a fundamental challenge to this longstanding narrative of knowledge. In one way or another they have begun to question the causal sequence at the heart of the empiricist account: that theoretical propositions are driven or determined by real-world properties. It is precisely this causal sequence that permits the conclusion that theories can accurately map reality and be used for purposes of prediction and control. However, as the irreverent chorus has begun to assemble, the causal sequence has been *reversed*: as we find, it is the process of theorizing that engenders what we take to be properties of the real world. Theories do not mirror reality; they are products of human interchange.

Early signals of the revolution appeared in the writings of Wittgenstein and others in the ordinary language tradition. All that may be said of the mental world, proposed Wittgenstein, is already locked into the linguistic conventions of the culture. It is not the reality of the mind that constrains our theories of the mental world, but linguistic convention. And, as philosophers from Austin and Ryle to Rorty have demonstrated, such language conventions often lead us into asking misleading and ultimately fruitless questions concerning, for example, how reality comes to be represented in the mind. The revolutionary shift was also evident in history-of-science writings, where theorists such as Thomas Kuhn argued that revolutions in scientific theory are not driven by accretion in fact. Rather, they are fostered by Gestalt-like shifts in the perception of relevant facts. It is not the facts that drive theorists, but the perspectives of scientists that determine what counts as fact. Although Kuhn failed to make good on the radical implications of this early view, these implications have since been amplified in the work of

Feyerabend and others on scientific revolution.

In the field of sociology, the emergence of labelling theory, ethno-methodology, and the sociology of knowledge also began to play out the same theme. From the standpoint of labelling theory and ethnomethodology, what we take to be the facts of social deviance, suicide and the like are not the results of such events in themselves; rather the existing forestructure of labels or methods for socially negotiating reality determine what counts as deviance, suicide, and the like. For sociologists of knowledge this has meant that the scientific laboratory becomes a focus of research interest: what are the social processes at play in the laboratory that produce what we take to be the realities of science?

Post-structuralist thought echoes such work in a different way. Structuralists such as Lévi-Strauss and Chomsky had argued that our means of defining reality are limited by internal dispositions or mental makeup. However, post-structuralist writings have generally externalized these limitations. That is, rather than mental limitations imposed upon language, linguistic limitations are forced upon the mind. These limitations in language are then traced to the social order. For example, Foucault proposed that our understandings of nature, social life, and knowledge at any point are limited by a pervasive, culturally specific *episteme*–or conditions of knowledge making. These conditions are intimately connected with various forms of social practice–including power relations.

Contemporary literary and hermeneutic theory expands on these themes. Inquiry into what are called "reader effects" in literary study has dominated much recent thinking. As theorists such as Stanley Fish have argued, what a text says is less the product of its own inherent properties than of the predispositions brought to the text by the reader. Theoretically, then, the same literary work is open to as many different interpretations as there are readers. For literary thinkers in the deconstructionist mode this line of thinking is carried to its extreme. As Derrida, DeMan and others propose, writing is not mimetic; it fails to describe a world independent of itself. Rather, critical or expository writing is governed by rules for its own construction; as it is said, writing is self-referring. In this way the supposed object of the writing is deconstructed. A similar theme is amplified by historiographers such as Louis Mink and Hayden Whyte. As they propose, the writing of history is largely governed by rules of narrative composition. It is thus the literary form that dominates our sense of historical reality. Semiotic analysts expand on this perspective by documenting a variety of literary figures or tropes (metaphor, metonomy, etc.) which are employed to construct realistic writing. In effect, the sense of reality conveyed by a text (or research paper) is, in this case, the product not of reality itself, but of an array of literary devices.

Recent inquiry in both psychology and anthropology furnish additional insights as they explore the ways in which understandings of self, others, and world vary across time and culture. As it is demonstrated, how we think of the child's capacities, the adult's personality, the nature of emotion, the nature of mental functioning, and so on are historically situated constructions with a certain functional value for societies at a given time. Similarly, in communication theory there has been a vital renaissance of interest in the works of Kenneth Burke, Wayne Booth and others concerned with the use of rhetoric in generating intelligibility. Others have turned their attention increasingly to the ways in which meanings are negotiated or managed over time; the sense of reality in this mode is the result of relationships among persons.

Such themes have been employed more critically by Marxists, feminists and humanist scholars more generally. In this case the attempt has been to demonstrate that various seemingly neutral and established scientific assumptions are value interested. Rather than reflecting the state of nature, scientists have perhaps unwittingly sustained views that furthered their own investments. As critical theorists demonstrate, much social theory serves to maintain an oppressive social order (in which scientists typically occupy a privileged position); feminist theorists demonstrate how existing accounts in biology, psychology and history favour male supremacy. Similar kinds of arguments have revealed within existing theories implicit racism, ageism, ethnocentrism and the like.

In all these cases–from Wittgenstein, through the sociology of science, post-structuralism, hermeneutics, literary theory, semiotics, and on through inquiry in psychology, anthropology, communications theory and modern critical analysis–the message is repeated: Theories about the world are not representational or mimetic, but the result of human interchange or construction.

For many this emergent view of knowledge as social construction has invited a new and exciting dialogue. Traditional disciplinary boundaries have been torn asunder as scholars have sought to exchange views with those who have arrived at similar ends from disparate paths. How much is shared, where are the differences, how powerful are the emerging arguments, what are their limits? All such questions demand colloquy of the broadest sort. And the excitement of such dialogue is fired to fever pitch by the emerging consciousness that its participants may be in the process of performing an intellectual checkmate. In the game of competing ideas this reversal in causal sequence is a form of master stroke. It has long been the major preoccupation of most scientific (if not academic) disciplines over the past century to develop, engender and proclaim the possession of knowledge, descriptions and explanations that represent the world in an accurate fashion. Yet, from the confluence of arguments I have just outlined, the warrant for such proclamations of knowledge is fully jeopardized. From the constructionist standpoint these bodies of so-called knowledge are not mirrors or maps of an independent reality, but the result of social negotiation, rules of procedure, literary tropes, rhetorical strategems and the like. The sciences (and related disciplines) are thus robbed of their capacity to claim truth or knowledge; the world to which they refer is deconstructed, and they are left with only a thin veil of rhetorical justification. Further, as the established disciplines come tumbling down one upon the other, who steps forward from the debris to proclaim the final victory but those who have advanced various forms of the social constructionist thesis, who have seen through the humbug, broken through the ontological sham, and have dared to pull the rug from under truth and knowledge. And it is the social constructionist who understands the craft of knowledge making–of constructing compelling realities.

For many scholars these are dramatic times. The twilight of the empiricist worldview appears rapidly approaching. In its stead there is emerging a new vision of knowledge, one that embeds it within social process. But let us continue to play out the scenario. Are we on the edge of a truly profound disjunction in Western thought, or are we merely experiencing a child's temporary enthusiasm with a new toy? After all, there is much to favour the continuation of the empiricist paradigm. Its practitioners have become skilled in its deployment; criteria of evaluation have been established; status hierarchies are dependent upon its mastery; granting agencies invite its continuation; most of the major journals are designed for its expression; and with the claim of being an "empirical science" one enjoys a certain degree of public trust and respect. So what if there is no intellectual justification; so what if the entire edifice is misleading; and so what if it cannot make good on its promises? In terms of power, prestige and funding it remains the best game in town. And to abandon it is to purchase a fare on a perilous roller coaster with unsure destination. In good conscience, I cannot encourage the young, aspiring social scientist to take the ride. In a time of brisk competition for academic positions the deviant or decrier is among the first to be sacrificed. It is a ride for the rugged, those tolerant of uncertainty, and perhaps for those who feel with Nietzsche that one must live dangerously for it is the only time one lives at all.

It is my view that if the constructionist venture is to overcome the inertial force of the empiricist tradition, it must confront a series of arduous conceptual challenges. These challenges must be confronted if the present movement is to alter significantly the course of intellectual history. New forms of discourse are required, new intelligibilities, justifications, and options for practice. It is these challenges that can provide the newcomer with the possibility of significant accomplishment. They are also the kinds of challenges that must be of focal concern to a progressive, humanist social science. In the remaining pages I wish to share three of my chief concerns for the development of a mature constructionism.

The Reconstruction of Metatheory

As I have outlined, the behavioural movement in the social sciences has essentially lost its metatheoretical underpinnings. The justificatory foundations have been eroded. Further, one can discern amidst the smoke of continuing battle the emergence of a social constructionist phalanx. However, if you examine my review of constructionist work more closely you will find that it has largely been of a critical variety. That is, in one discipline after the other it is demonstrated that what has previously been taken to be data-driven knowledge is more reasonably viewed as a product of the community of knowledge makers. The data have not driven theory, so much as in the social process of negotiating theory the data have been created as rhetorical supports. Yet, although there is broad deployment of a social constructionist strategy in dismantling long-standing traditions, as yet there is little in the way of an articulated theory of socially constructed knowledge. Empiricist metatheory does not yet have a fully developed competitor in the form of a body of constructionist metatheory–or theory of knowledge. Until the suppositions underlying the constructionist critique are fully articulated and examined, we cannot determine the potential viability of the movement.

There are at least two critical questions which such metatheory must be prepared to address. The first is the notorious problem of self-justification. If constructionists succeed in deconstructing the object of knowledge in all the established disciplines, on what grounds is one to claim that constructionist inquiry itself possesses an object? On its own account, are not constructionists simply engaging in a series of conventional or rhetorical exercises which are themselves without objects? How is it that previous disciplines have no object while constructionists do? This is no small question, for until an answer can be provided, the force of the constructionist argument is severely blunted. If constructionism has an object of study (mapping the contours of social construction), then so do the empiricist accounts of the world. If social constructionist analysis is without an object, then why should one pay attention? Why is it not merely engendering talk? Further, while the established sciences can send rockets to the moon, discover oil, or predict the birth rate, constructionists are left with only a wagging of tongues. The position is indeed precarious.

Required by a constructionist metatheory is essentially a new theory of reference. It is insufficient to demonstrate that words are not mimetic

devices; required is a positive statement that would enable us to understand why it has been so captivating to believe that they are. Further,
such an explanation should not simultaneously discredit the constructionist enterprise. For example, one must be able to give an account as
to why it is that a rocket engineer's statement that the space shuttle will
or will not reach orbit is not merely poetics; such words do make a
difference to what happens next in people's lives (or deaths). The same
is true of the doctor's diagnosis of cancer. Such verbalizations may not
be mirrors or maps, but at the same time they cannot be reduced to
rhetoric or discourse alone.

I am presently ill equipped to provide a fully developed alternative to
existing theories of reference. It is my considered opinion, however, that
the solution will lie somewhere in the domain of linguistic pragmatics.
That is, we may view language utterances as integers in broader patterns
of action. As such patterns emerge and are stabilized in a culture (or
subculture), each integer becomes an anticipatory signal for that which
follows. Thus words become devices enabling the pattern to be successfully completed. Using grammar as an illustration, if I say "John hit...,"
you may justifiably anticipate the appearance of a third term, an object
as it were ("the ball" or "the attacker"), to follow subject and verb. In
the same way, if I announce that the space shuttle "will fly successfully,"
this utterance has pragmatic implications for what happens when NASA
officials do things that we call "give orders" and engineers engage in
what we call "launching the rocket." If we take this pragmatic orientation, we are able to retain the position that theories of the world are not
ontological guides or maps; the sciences (and related disciplines) do not
inform us of reality. Their mistake has been to objectify the pragmatic
implements. At the same time, this perspective enables us to say that the
words of scientists, and of constructionist analysis, can and do play
important pragmatic functions. For example, constructionists can
perform demonstrations of the utility of various rhetorical strategies in
creating a sense of reality, while at the same time not proclaiming the
truth of such analyses. It is not that constructionist accounts map reality,
in this case, but its accounts can be useful signalling devices within the
social production of what are taken to be true statements.

Yet, a constructionist theory must do more than solve the problem of
self-justification. Ideally such a metatheory would furnish a conception of
progress, along with a companionate account of criteria of evaluation.
Thus far constructionist analysis has been employed primarily as a means
of undermining established authority. The proclaimer of knowledge is
brought low. Yet, to follow the lines of the preceding analysis, constructionists cannot play the part of spoiler unless others are willing to serve
as foils. In effect, the position constructionists now find themselves in is
essentially parasitic. As many believe, this is indeed the position that

deconstructionist literary theory has reached. Like solipsism, it is a supportable position; however, once you have layed claim to this position, productive dialogue is at an end. Once we have moved to the checkmate of social construction the game is finished. Required, then, is a conception of constructionist analysis in which more positive or progressive goals are envisioned.

Let me expand the view of linguistic pragmatics to see how such an end might be accomplished. As we see, there is little merit in the idea of scientific progress as the accumulation of ever more accurate propositional sets. It seems to me that we require a more Hegelian concept of progress, in which self-reflexivity replaces certainty. We should honour those positions that serve to make us aware of the problems inherent in positions previously held. As each critique is elaborated it will lay the grounds for a new ontology–which itself stands to be shorn of its ostensive grounding. In effect, we require a view of progress in which the continuous erosion of confidence and emancipation from the strangulating assumptions of "the real" are the endpoints. Elsewhere I have proposed the concept of generativity as the essential criterion of evaluation. It is the generative theory which most departs from the accepted conventions of intelligibility, and in so doing throws reality into question and opens new potentials for action and growth. In this sense we must honour the theories of Marx, Freud and even Skinner–not because they are accurate, but because they were generative theories. They succeeded in undermining the certainties of the time and generating alternative forms of action.

At the same time, I do not think the generative criterion takes us far enough in the evaluation of competing theories. In particular, I believe constructionists are in the position to reinstate a form of discourse that has been systematically omitted from the traditional empiricist account of knowledge. From the empiricist perspective the production of knowledge is dispassionate; the accurate mirror possesses no values, no motives, and no ideals other than that of verisimilitude. Yet, as has become progressively clear, the language of the sciences cannot be expunged of value; and in particular, descriptions and explanations of human action are inherently and inextricably impregnated with visions of the good. Rather than viewing such value saturation as an embarrassing *hazard de parcours*, it seems to me that we are in a position to turn this liability into an advantage. Valuational terms are some of the most powerful pragmatic implements in western culture. Terms such as *immoral, unfair, exploitative, inhumane* and the like can have enormous social consequences. Rather than removing such terms from the vocabulary of the serious scholar, there is much to be gained by their reinstatement.

Such valuational refurbishment seems particularly invited by the kind of pragmatic account of theoretical discourse suggested in the preceding. If we view theories not as reflections but as constituents of ongoing sequences of action, then social theory has implications for social pattern. For example, theories of person blame have different economic, political and legal implications than theories that hold social systems (and not persons) responsible for patterns of human conduct. To favour a theory, then, is to favour various forms of social life. In what terms are these forms of social life to be assessed? It seems to me that the language of human values should play an essential role. The valuational implications of competing theoretical commitments should come to play a role as important as that previously assigned to "facts." The kind of valuational assessments that critical theorists and feminists, for example, have learned to do so well should become part of the normal set of questions asked of a theoretical position.

Mediation and the Development of Communication

From a fully elaborated constructionist standpoint, all claims to truth are "essentially contestable." One cannot possess standards of certainty that lie outside the domain of human negotiation. This condition confronts us with important questions concerning the adjudication of competing claims. If one government constructs its actions as defensive while another sees the same actions as aggressive, if one political party sees a law as unjust while another sees it as essential to a strong economy, and if one professional group holds that people are subject to unconscious impulses while another views human action as the result of conscious choice, how are we to reach solutions? There is now no court of facts to which we can appeal–nor, as may be pointed out, was there ever really such. It is insufficient to fall back on Grecian formulas for clarity in communication, nor does Habermas's analysis of communicative action fully solve the problem. Interlocutors may be fully transparent and possess equal degrees of power and still remain locked in disagreement. Feyerabend's analysis of open negotiation in a free society is helpful, but offers no protection from the very form of uncompromising invective in which he himself so often indulges. New theories of community are required, theories that might explore the possibility of fundamental and inextricable interdependence of competing claims.

In pursuing enlightenment regarding the mediation of disputes, there is a related problem requiring closest attention, that of human communication. From the traditional standpoint, language is largely a product of our mental representations. It contains the results of our observations and rational derivations–both assumed to be mental processes. Speaking (or writing) is thus not important in itself (such activities would only be a collection of assorted sounds or markings); it is the mental state of the speaker or writer that is ultimately of interest. In effect, the process of reading or listening is traditionally viewed as one in which we attempt to ascertain the underlying intentions of the other. Communication is a form of intersubjectivity. Again, however, we find that from the constructionist perspective this view of communication proves deeply problematic. If words do not reflect alternative realities, in what sense are they reflections of mental states? And if language about minds is properly deconstructed, what advantage is there in assuming the independent existence of the mental states which language putatively expresses? If there are, in fact, no mental states, then how can language represent them? And if language is not used for such purposes, then human communication is not a matter of drawing inferences from surface manifestations to internal intentions. In effect, we find that when the constructionist orientation is pushed to its logical conclusion, the traditional account of human communication as intersubjective connection is untenable.

It is my belief that a reinterpretation of communicative acts can be derived from a consideration of language as social pragmatics. In particular, we may view communication as essentially the process of coordinating actions–in this case verbal (although verbal language is a limiting case). That is, my words are sensible (or sense making) only in the degree to which they approximate existing patterns of interchange. The extreme case is the foreign language; we fail to comprehend not because we cannot ascertain the mental states of the foreigner but because his or her particular execution of sounds fails to duplicate the broader patterns in which our own language is embedded. There are no direct translations of foreign words because the meaning of any word is given in large measure by its context of reiterative usage. And in the case of our own language, if you ask me what I mean by a given utterance, there is little reason to suppose that you wish to have a report on the state of my cortex. Rather, this is a signal that additional discourse is required in order that the broader pattern of interchange can be clarified.

Let me illustrate with reference to the communication of emotional states. We have traditionally viewed the emotions as mental events, and our emotional predicates (e.g., "I feel happy," "I am depressed," "You make me angry") as vehicles for expressing these internal states. However, as the present analysis suggests, these terms are not maps of an internal region. My knowledge of you cannot be reduced to propositions about your internal condition. When you communicate I am not trying to draw inferences from the surface to an internal reality. Rather, emotion terms may be viewed as components of a more elaborated dance of meaning in which at least two persons are a part.

In our own inquiry on this topic we have asked persons how they would respond to various expressions of emotion. It is rapidly discerned that there are important cultural constraints on these replies. If a friend tells you he or she is depressed, there are only a handful of conversational moves that will allow you to "make sense" by contemporary cultural standards. And if you then ask additional research participants (now playing the part of the depressed person) how they would respond to these various reactions, you find again that there are only a small number of meaningful moves. If this research procedure is followed out, you find that emotional expressions form parts of elaborate scenarios (or *relational narratives*, as we have called them). They are constituent parts of stories that require at least two participants to complete, and completion is typically the "happy ending" of the Aristotelian comedy. In effect, emotion terms are embedded within relational forms. Love, anger, sadness and the like are parts of cultural performances coordinated by two or more actors. Knowledge of emotion is not a plumbing of internal depths so much as an interactional achievement.

Innovation in Praxis

Thus far I have touched on a series of impending conceptual puzzles and have suggested avenues of possible solution. However, if constructionism is to be a truly revolutionary force, more will be required than conceptual innovation. Constructionism should make a difference to the culture, both in terms of scientific practices and in terms of patterns of social life. If constructionist inquiry serves only to criticize and reinterpret, it slowly becomes a form of linguistic idealism. Further consideration must be given to the problem of praxis.

In considering alterations in praxis let us first cast an eye to our colleagues in the natural sciences. In particular, how are we to consider the technological advances of which they so proudly boast? There is a strong temptation to employ such advances as evidence on behalf of the empiricist worldview; does the harnessing of electricity, the atom, and the gene not demonstrate the power of testing empirical hypotheses? Should the social sciences not continue to be informed by natural-science methods and metatheory? Although the arguments are too extensive to elaborate at this juncture, post-empiricist thought of the kind previously outlined does make it clear that whatever gains are being made in the technology, they are not the result of the assiduous application of empiricist rules of method. Natural-science theory can neither be derived from data nor do such theories themselves enable one to derive deductions for subsequent action. Or, to put it another way, technological advances bear in no way on the truth or falsity of the relevant theories.

This is to say that the success of a steam engine, an electric generator or a turbojet is no different in principle than the success of a sonnet or an oil painting. Each requires an immersion in a series of skilled practices–not reducible to or describable in words. The chief function of theories within the natural sciences may well be to enable the community of scientists to organize itself more effectively around these practices.

Now let us turn more directly to the social sciences. There is nothing within the constructionist perspective that would argue against the use of various mensurational and statistical techniques to aid in the process of social prediction. There are valuable social functions to be served in being able to predict what we call rates of crime, birth, divorce, and so on, or in plotting public reactions to various policies and persons. As in the natural sciences, these actuarial crafts offer the society many advantages. However, just as in the natural-science case, we should not confuse the words used to accompany the predictions with mirrors of the truth. What is to be said of the vast range of what is usually termed "pure research" in the social sciences, the laboratory experiments, multiple regression analyses, longitudinal analyses, cross-lagged panels, cohort analyses, and the like? Do they have sustaining merit? Yes, to an extent, but not for the reasons traditionally furnished. From the constructionist perspective it is misleading to propose that such research bears in any important way on the truth value of any hypothesis. To speak of data is to construct the world in a particular way; all data are theoretically saturated and infinitely defeasible. However, this does not mean that such research is wholly obviated. It is appropriate to view such work as furnishing rhetorical power to one's theory rather than empirical justification. Data are like paintings or photographs; they help to illustrate or vivify one's theoretical accounts and thereby render them more compelling.

From the constructionist standpoint the collection of data should be placed in a role ancillary to that of developing coherent and socially significant theory. For all too long method has reigned superior to theory in the social sciences, and the result is a rather impoverished and often banal array of theoretical intelligibilities. The time is at hand to reverse this hierarchy and place the major emphasis on developing social praxis. Theoretical assumptions about human nature and action pervade the common discourse, and are used in carrying out social life. As social-science theory is articulated and disseminated within the culture, it enters into the cultural practices–to alter them for good or ill. Concepts such as *instinct*, *inferiority complex*, *economic class*, and *stress* are only a few of the more prominent examples.

The constructionist challenge for the social sciences is thus to develop theories that can facilitate the kind of social action one believes will contribute to the good society. Such theoretical work may be critical, but it may also be constructive, demonstrating promising courses of action along with supportive rationales. Marxist theory furnished an intelligibility that moved millions. Similarly, social thinkers have helped to furnish rationales for action to the black minority, the anti-war movement, feminists, and many others. We are only beginning to appreciate the power of well constructed theories to transform social life. It is staggering to consider how history might have been changed if all the intelligence devoted to developing and deploying methods and statistics had instead been devoted to generating intelligibilities for those in need.

As constructionism advances, we should also anticipate diminishing interest in research methods of manipulation and control. For many, such methods are themselves morally suspect–suggesting as they do that our most intimate knowledge of others is secured through forms of dispassionate, alienated and demeaning manipulation. At the same time, we might hope to see the flourishing of alternative methodological orientations. In this case methods are not employed for purposes of furnishing empirical warrants. Rather, such methods might aid in the generative process of theoretical growth. At the present time a number of social scientists are attempting to develop dialogic research methods–practices in which researcher and participant engage in ongoing interchange, with an eye toward enhancing the conceptual resources of all. As it is hoped, such research can serve an emancipatory function. It should enable its participants to break through the conventionalized realities and to see them in the context of alternatives. The research process is thus aimed at enhancing choice for all concerned.

In summary, my attempt has been to sketch the contours of what is rapidly becoming a major intellectual force within Western culture, to demonstrate why it is an important force, and to indicate some of its major challenges for the future. In doing so I may have succeeded in alienating many readers. However, if I have succeeded at all in challenging your imagination, perhaps you have glimpsed, with me, the possibility for what may be called a "new enlightenment." Enlightenment thinking from the seventeenth century to the present has succeeded in wresting authority from church and divinely sanctioned government. It has done so by its emphasis on reason and evidence. In this way, it was believed, authority could be disseminated among the people. With the use of private faculties for reason and observation, each individual possessed the ability to reign (like a pope or king) over his or her own life. However, as history has moved on, it is the sciences that have gained the corner on reason and objectivity. Through complex theory, sanctified methodology, and rarefied statistical practices, they have laid claim to authority of knowledge and technological advance. The palaces of plenty now belong to the sciences. The populace has again lost voice. However, should the constructionist enterprise meet the kinds of challenges outlined here, there is promise of a new enlightenment. The construction of reality is, after all, a communal responsibility. All voices have the potential to enrich. In the end we are forced to rely on ourselves alone; we are alone with each other—no voice of God, no final court, no incorrigible truth to rescue us from our own designs. With awareness of the interdependent nature of our truths, perhaps we can reduce the threat of mutual annihilation and begin to achieve community.

2

A PLEA FOR THE CATEGORIES

David MacGregor

Over thirty years ago Harold A. Innis wrote that "Culture is concerned with the capacity of the individual to appraise problems in terms of time and space and with enabling him to take the proper steps at the right time. It is at this point that the tragedy of modern culture has arisen as inventions in commercialism have destroyed a sense of time." The tragedy of culture Innis spoke of in "A Plea for Time" has in many respects advanced much further than perhaps even he would have dreamt possible. He lamented that the social sciences had become increasingly concerned with topical problems and that social-science departments had become schools of journalism. He expressed fear that if government took as strong an interest in social science as it did in the so-called hard sciences, "the social sciences will be on hand with the most beautifully developed projects for research that federal money can buy." Innis described a tendency of the universities to justify themselves to the community by their value to business or to other extremely worthy causes. "Culture," he pointed out, "is not concerned with these questions."[1] The real object of the universities and the culture they nourish is the development of thought.

In the age of the computer, the effortless gathering of data has almost smothered the instinct to theorize. "Why think about it if it can't be measured?"–this has become the cry of a generation. And when the loud caravan of hasty empiricism at last disappears down the highway of science it is followed by its entourage of even hastier philosophical summations and judgments that make a point of denying the relationship between thought and the universe. The sign is a circle that like the tape worm eventually devours itself.

"Philosophy and commonsense," commented Hegel in the Preface to the *Science of Logic*–where like Innis he noted a contemporary demand for attention to "immediate requirements" and practical skills for public and private life–"thus co-operating to bring about the downfall of metaphysics, there was seen the strange spectacle of a cultured nation without metaphysics–like a temple richly ornamented in other respects but without a holy of holies."[2] If in Hegel's time the condition of metaphysics was desperate, in our own period metaphysics has replaced alchemy as the dodo of intellectual endeavour.

I was kindly invited by the organizers of a landmark conference to present my ideas on the formulation of "guidelines for doing social science well in our time." Unlike the other speakers at the conference, who had completed pathbreaking "substantive work informed by a humanist approach," I was to speak as an obscure spinner of theories, a trifling artisan of the metaphysical. Nevertheless, I had the hubris to accept the invitation "to formulate guidelines...deductively, from the opposite direction" of empirical fact. You will forgive me if I compare myself in this respect only, to the great G. B. Shaw who observed in a letter to H. G. Wells: "The longer I live the more I see that I am never wrong about anything, and that all the pains I have so humbly taken to verify my notions have only wasted my time."[3] Here as elsewhere the great playwright and the founder of scientific socialism had much in common. In the appeal "to actual experience," Karl Marx contended in *Capital*, "the 'why and wherefore' of the matter remain a mystery."[4]

The social psychologist Leon Rappoport has noted an intriguing movement in present-day social science. Just when philosophy in its effort to make itself useful to natural science and computer studies has apparently given up the "infinite and the eternal," as Hegel described metaphysics, social scientists are taking up the torch of the absolute. "Pushed by a growing awareness of how their disciplines have been formed by unexamined epistemological assumptions," Rappoport declares, "social scientists are reentering the domains of philosophy, and...are in some instances beginning to dominate them."[5] Perhaps, then, it would not be inappropriate if the guidelines I suggest for "doing social science well in our time" contain a large dose of the metaphysical. I have called this paper, "A Plea for the Categories," and it would seem necessary, therefore, to present at the beginning some account of the categories, and why I believe their proper understanding is essential to the conduct of a humanist social science. "It is common," writes Steven Collins, "to find anthropologists, sociologists, intellectual historians and others, as well as philosophers, using the philosophical terminology of *categories of thought* to refer to the more or less fundamental ideas, concepts or simply patterns of thinking which are found in different cultures and different historical periods." In this usage–which contrasts strongly with the one I have in mind–the categories are relative and contingent, wholly derivable from their empirical, historic context. Their authority depends, at one extreme, on the claims of common sense and popular culture, and at the other, the demands of "vested economic, political, religious or other interests."[6]

The view I wish to argue for in this paper resembles that of Emile Durkheim, who suggested in *Elementary Forms of the Religious Life* that categories are not "very simple notions which the first comer can very easily arrange from his own personal observations," but are "priceless instruments of thought which human groups have laboriously forged through the centuries.... A complete section of the history of humanity is resumed therein."[7] The categories have their origin in social life; but far from being arbitrary and contingent, they together constitute what it means to be human. Durkheim's understanding of the categories flowed from the radical individualism of Immanuel Kant and the philosophical sociology of Hegel.[8] Kant developed his doctrine as a response to David Hume's persuasive critique of the notion of cause and effect, the idea of "necessary connection." Hume observed that "cause and effect" cannot be found anywhere in the external world; rather they are entities imposed by mind in order to grasp the nature of witnessed phenomena. Much impressed by Hume's criticism, as well as the Scottish philosopher's insistence that only empirical facts are worth talking about, Kant wrote the *Critique of Pure Reason*. There he proposed that the categories employed by science are not a result of observation, but are worked up beforehand, or *a priori*, and then applied to the empirical world. Karl Popper has nicely summarized the Kantian project: "that *the world as we know it is our interpretation of the observable facts in the light of theories that we ourselves invent*."[9]

Kant's critique struck a double blow. He at once expelled metaphysics from the realm of science, and pulled the rug out from under the dominant scientific modes of empiricism and materialism. Thought is active and creative, Kant argued, but only so long as it restricts itself to the world of experience. If science involves itself with metaphysical, transcendental ideas of pure Reason, like God and the soul, it becomes transcendent, losing itself in contradiction and unavoidable illusion.

The delusions of metaphysics, however, are no worse than those of empiricism, which imagines science has only to describe the world as it is perceived by the senses in order to confront reality. For Kant, crude sensation is an entirely unreliable guide to the character of the universe. Sensations are purely subjective, prey to happenstance and fleeting conditions. A drunk person certainly has sensations; they are at least as compelling as any that individual might experience when sober. Yet they may be entirely false. The separation of dream from reality can only be achieved through employment of intersubjectively valid categories, like space and time, cause and effect. With proper use of the categories our sensations can be tamed so that what they show us is indeed what has actually transpired.

The conditions for the possibility of experience, says Kant, are provided by the ego or I–the transcendental unity of self-consciousness–which unites the manifold content offered by sensation with and through the categories of thought.

Paradoxically, the Kantian categories are wholly impotent. They have no content in themselves, supplying only the form to a vibrant, living reality. "[H]aving got rid of the dark utterances of metaphysics," notes Hegel, "of the colourless communion of spirit with itself, outer existence seemed to be transformed into the bright world of flowers–and there are no *black* flowers, as we know."[10] In Kant's philosophy, reality remains forever external to us, because the categories do not present the world as it is in itself, but only as human beings perceive it. Conceivably, a being with a different set of sensations and an alternative battery of categories might experience things in a completely different way.

There is hardly a single element in Hegel that is not foreshadowed in Kant. Hegel paid close and sympathetic attention to the Königsburg thinker. The doctrine of the categories in particular had an over-whelming importance for him. Nevertheless, he rejected Kant's theory as a monstrosity, a violation of the human essence. Kant starts out to restore the supremacy of spirit, of mind; he labours to prove the funda-mental place of thought in science and human endeavour. In the end, however, he strips thought of its powers and reimposes the barrier between thinking and its object in an even grosser form than it previ-ously had attained. What greater alienation is possible than this: "Kant," Hegel remarks, "Kant...holds that what we think is false because it is we who think it."[11]

Kant's gigantic efforts appeared to turn science upside down; but when he was finished the whole edifice stood quite the same as it did before. In place of a critical examination, Kant took the categories as he found them in textbooks on logic. He made no attempt to discover their inner relationship or the secret of their development. Nor did he survey the vast interconnections between logic and nature, or between systems of thought and the social world. This Hegel accepted as his task–a project that remains as vital to the progress of a humanist social science today as it ever did. "Hegel," writes Terry Pinkard, "is not simply some nineteenth-century German romantic listening to his own incantations of the World Spirit but a philosopher concerned with carefully working out the logical relations between all the different ways in which we experi-ence things and talk about that experience."[12]

Hegel calls empiricism and the putative advance from this mode of thought accomplished by Kant, the "understanding consciousness." It is characterized by two central defects. The "limited and partial" categories of the understanding assume a disjunction, a split between reality and mind, which fails to reflect on its own operations. For the understanding consciousness, the external world is on one side, thought on the other; and the problem is to twist and wrench thinking to correspond to perceived reality. (Note that this is what "good science" does; "bad science" twists and distorts reality to conform with its own preconcep-tions.) Secondly, the categories "are always of restricted content, and so persist in antithesis to one another and still more to the Absolute." The understanding accepts its categories unaltered from common sense and formal logic, and applies them willy-nilly to the object under investigation. Little attention is paid to the relationship between the categories and their relative power to comprehend the level of reality to which they are applied. Moreover, the objects for study themselves are selected at random or at the whim of the observer; the interconnections between objects are left out of consideration.[13]

If the categories are inadequate in face of the complexity of the empirical world, they are completely irrelevant for any consideration of "the Absolute." Questions about God, Freedom, the Soul, and so forth, are systematically excluded by the understanding consciousness, or at least restricted to a subordinate role. The great political philosopher, John Plamenatz, noted that the problems raised by political theory are precisely the kind beyond the range of science. "Political theorizing is thus, on [his] view, an exemplification of the project of metaphysical self-knowledge." Reliance on limited scientific categories places social science researchers at a serious disadvantage. As Alisdair MacIntyre suggests, "a social order is generally understood by those who inhabit it as standing in certain relationships to nature and to the divine. Nature is understood as providing some particular kind of environment, a source of fears, threats, and hopes, of material for enjoyment or domination or awe: the divine is either an important part of the natural and social orders, altogether distinct from either or both, or absent or non-existent. Ordinary members of almost all societies are metaphysicians in their implicit and explicit theorizing, a luxury which the Western academic tradition denies to social scientists."[14]

In contrast to the external and finite categories of the understanding, the Hegelian category–the Notion, as Hegel calls it–is the self-conscious individual *and* the individual's relationship to the universe and to herself or himself. "[T]he category means this, that existence and self-consciousness are the same being, the same not as a matter of comparison, but really and truly in and for themselves."[15] Human consciousness does not "possess" categories as you and I possess a coat or a hat. We are what we are, human beings, because we think; and the individual is above all a being of thought, a universe of categories. As Hegel remarks, "the soul is virtually the totality of nature: as an individual soul it is a monad: it is itself the explicitly put totality of its particular world–that world being included in it and filling it up; and to that world it stands but as to itself."[16]

The system of categories is the subject of Hegel's *Science of Logic*, which is composed of three moments or spheres of thought: being, essence and the notion. The sphere of Being concerns single things, their inner duality and relationships; it deals with the properties of objects, their determination, i.e. how many? what ratio? and so forth.

Essence deals with processes among things; it is the moment in which the categories of Being are employed to trace the connections between objects. In this region of thought, the thing is reflected upon and variously related to other things with categories like cause and effect, reciprocity, necessity. Essence is the world of the dead, because it is essentially passive, without personality, always dependent on something else. This is the universe of appearance, of laws, the specification of invariant relationships.

The sphere of the Notion is the bright circle of personality, the life and thought of the social individual. The Notion embraces the vitality, and interconnections with others, of the individual subject; as such it is the triple sphere, the unity of opposites in a third thing, or to use the religious language Hegel was fond of, the region of the trinity. At the highest stage, the Notion stands for social life within the state, "the actuality of concrete freedom." Here, says Hegel, "the universal does not prevail or achieve completion except along with particular interests and through the co-operation of particular knowing and willing; and individuals likewise do not live as private persons for their own ends alone, but in the very act of willing these they will the universal in the light of the universal, and their activity is consciously aimed at none but the universal end."[17]

"The whole of Philosophy," Hegel remarks, "...resembles a circle of circles."[18] The progress of *Logic* is the movement of thought, its self-development outwards, and also its inner self-penetration. Each stage represents a necessary movement forward of the logical concept, but also a doubling backward, a recovery of the inner richness of what went before. Hegel calls this double movement *aufheben* (to put by, or set aside). This term means both to supercede or go beyond the subject at hand, and also to preserve it, to keep its special principle. The relation of Hegelian philosophy to that of Kant provides an important example of this process of development through contradiction.

Logic is consciousness reflecting on itself, as Hegel contends; but the movement of the categories retraces the evolution of thought in the history of philosophy.[19] Being and nothing, for example, are the primary concepts of the earliest Eastern thought systems. The advance represented by the category of becoming, which encompasses the unity and dissolution of being and nothing, belongs to the mind of the ancient Greeks. In the history of philosophy, the growth of the categories is *partly accidental* instead of *purely logical*; certain mental productions appear and are carried forward; others are lost and dwindle away to be rediscovered later on; categories properly dependent upon earlier ones are sometimes elaborated first, and so forth.

Most important, the appearance and development of the categories is no work of some ethereal, detached mind. The categories summarize and inform human experience; their conscious development in philosophy is made possible by their prior origination in the vast inarticulateness of everyday social life. To recapitulate the life of the categories is also to embark on a concrete, materialist examination of the human project.

The social scientist who took most seriously the categories as Hegel understood them was, of course, Marx. The entire structure of Volume One of *Capital*–the only part of that seminal work Marx himself completed–is laid out on the logical pattern. Thus if *Logic* begins with alternation between opposites in the initial unity of thought–Being and Nothing–and their conversion into Becoming, *Capital* starts with the polar opposites of use-value and exchange-value which make up the unity called the commodity. These opposites in turn dissolve into the process of exchange–the Becoming, as it were, of bourgeois society.

From another angle, the opening passages of *Capital* are a reconstruction of the initial sections of Hegel's *Philosophy of Right*, which begins with the opposites, abstract personality and the thing or commodity, and continues with the categories of property, possession, use, alienation and contract. Perhaps it is significant to observe in this context that Hegel and Marx chose opposite starting points in their analysis of society. Marx begins with the thing, the commodity; Hegel opens with the individual human being, abstract personality. Nevertheless, Hegel makes it exceedingly clear very early on that if human personality is of infinite importance, eternal relevance, it becomes in bourgeois society no more than a thing, a commodity, something to be bought and sold.

Marx carefully delineated the stages of his presentation in *Capital* in order to demonstrate as powerfully as possible the innermost drive of bourgeois society. For example, he sharply distinguishes the nature and capabilities of machinery from the actual employment of technology under capitalism. Thus he shows how the marvelous labour-saving inventions in the British textile industry turned out, through a "dialectical inversion," to be sure means of lengthening the workday and drawing hordes of ragged infants and children into the mills and factories of early nineteenth-century England.[20] In this way, he avoided the common misconception that technology itself is encumbered with certain "iron lusts" and "disk drives" that somehow compel it to degrade humanity. This compulsion lies in the cold heart of capital, where for a certain return on the dollar anything goes, including any moral residuals.

One of the many unforgettable moments in *Capital* comes when Marx discusses the theory of "abstinence," devised by "vulgar political economy" to explain the origin of interest and profit. According to this theory, profit does not arise–as the classical political economists like Smith and Ricardo contended–from the labour of the worker. Rather, profit is a function of the enterprise of the capitalist, and interest is a product of the entrepreneur's ability to "wait" for a return on investment. On the rare occasions when the nature of profit is discussed by contemporary economists–instead of shibboleths like "marginal productivity of capital," etc.–this remains a popular explanation, and everywhere in our society capitalists are congratulated on their wondrous ability to "take risks" and "create jobs."[21] Entrepreneurs could, after all, throw their money away playing Loto-Canada or skiing in Banff; instead they place their hard-earned cash in "the future," and thereby earn the respect and admiration of all. The asceticism of the banks, for example, where profit rates strain for triple digits, is a deep source of national pride.

Marx poured scorn on the substitution by vulgar political economy of "a sycophantic phrase" for "an economic category." If by investing his or her capital the businessperson displays "abstinence," then, says Marx, "let him...console himself with the reflection that virtue is its own reward." Turning to Hegelian dialectics, Marx points out that doing anything is, by definition, abstinence from doing something else. "It has never occurred to the vulgar economist to make the simple reflection that every human action may be conceived as an 'abstinence' from its opposite. Eating is abstinence from fasting, walking is abstinence from standing still, working is abstinence from idling, idling is abstinence from working, etc."[22]

As Marx's discussion makes clear, however, "abstinence" is not only a "sycophantic phrase" but also a misplaced category. The vulgar economists succeeded in foisting a very low level category into the discussion of an extremely complex social phenomenon, the relation between capital, labour and profit. Employing inappropriate or inadequate categories to discuss social relationships is a common practice in modern social science. Let me give some examples.

A most disheartening illustration is found in economics, and in some fields of other disciplines, such as sociology, where attention to numerical functions, statistical relationships and computer models has driven out not only theory and metaphysics, but empirical study itself. They are prime examples of the Hegelian dialectical inversion. Initially, advanced studies in statistics were aimed at sophisticated manipulation of data, in order to come to valid conclusions about the empirical world. In economics, however, they soon took leave of facts altogether and soared into the heights of abstraction.

The Nobel Prize-winning mathematical economist Leontieff has recently called attention to the deterioration of his own discipline. "Page after page of professional economic journals," he writes, "are filled with mathematical formulas leading the reader from sets of more or less plausible but entirely arbitrary assumptions to precisely stated but irrelevant theoretical conclusions." In a study of articles published in *The American Economic Review* between March, 1977, and December, 1981, "Leontieff found, 54 percent of AER articles were 'mathematical models without any data.' Another 22 percent drew statistical references from data generated for some other purpose. Another 12 percent used analysis with no data. Half of one percent of the articles used direct empirical analysis of data generated by the author. Leontieff says that a more recent tabulation finds the trends unabated. 'We found exactly one piece of empirical research, and it was about the utility maximization of pigeons.'"[23]

Mathematics, even in its most advanced forms, is entirely inadequate for the comprehension of human social behaviour. Despite ingenious analogies to human relationships, it remains rooted in the elementary categories of number, quantum, mass, and so forth. The amazing power of the very first categories, Being and Nothing, lies behind the success of the computer and its binary code of one and zero, being and nothing. But however successful it may be in certain types of explanation, the world of mind, of spirit, races well ahead of mathematics.

Misuse of the categories is by no means confined to established, mainstream disciplines. Anti-establishment academic enterprises are equally susceptible to what I shall call category error. Where Marxism, for example, is not itself degenerating into linguistic analysis, econometric models, statistical manipulations, and so forth, it is a major victim of this intellectual disease. The debate around what Nicos Poulantzas called "the relative autonomy of the state" is instructive in this respect.

Poulantzas was reacting to the "instrumentalist" Marxist notion of the state. According to adherents of this theory, democratic government is a mere tool of the ruling class, which staffs it with its own personnel and directs it mainly to fulfill the interests of profit. Poulantzas's "relative autonomy" formula was meant to express the ability of the political realm to act independently of capitalist influence in order to increase its effectiveness as a protector of the existing system.[24] After his intervention a debate ensued on the role of the state and the degree of its independence from capitalist-dominated civil society. Despite the ingenuity of the participants in this controversy, the arguments were imprisoned by the paucity of the terms under which they were presented.

Poulantzas's conception of the state was an advance over the instrumentalist version, which depends entirely on the categories of cause and effect: given a certain desire or need on the part of the capitalist class, then the direction of the state will be known. However, the relative autonomy thesis gets no further than the somewhat less unsatisfactory category which Hegel calls, "Mechanism with Affinity." In this relation, "the other itself [in this case, the state] has direction and reference toward the external [i.e., capitalist-dominated civil society]. But this external object is similarly central in itself, and being so, is no less only referred towards the other centre; so that it no less has its centrality in the other.... [T]heir independence is derived from, and due to, their connections with each other, and therefore to their own want of stability."[25]

Given its mechanistic nature, the category of relative autonomy could as well apply to the relation between an engine and a thermostatically-controlled engine fan, as to the relation of state and civil society, and the Marxist debate proceeded along predictable lines. "The fan is not directly controlled by the engine, but is there to ensure its smooth performance, even if sometimes the fan reduces the overall thrust of the engine. The action of the fan is subject to environmental conditions which in the short run do not affect the engine, but which in the long term could cause it to overheat. The engine itself, of course, is powered by the explosive force of the struggle between spark and fuel."

Hegel defines human social life, its grand achievements in culture, knowledge and the state, as "the Idea that *relates itself to itself as Idea*, the universal that has universality for its determinateness and existence...."[26] A prerequisite for doing social research well in our time should be the simple recognition of the immensity of the human achievement. Drawing on the Kantian heritage of *critique*, social science prides itself on its critical abilities, its propensity to rip away the veil of pretense and reveal the gorgon face that lies just beneath the placid mask of the existing order. This must always be a vital part of social science; but it is not enough.

For what Hegel calls the finite sciences, to know the nature of the human being is to study its morbidities, its sicknesses. Physicians have gathered knowledge of the body through study of its malformations, its blockages, its disorders. Psychology concentrates on diseases of the mind, or the foibles and trivialities of personality. Economics focusses on the grasping selfishness of the individual amidst scarcity and limitation. Sociology too often insists on the nullity of human conduct, the false pretense of ideology, the deviousness of social control, the perfidy of the state. These pursuits are valuable, but they have added only a little to genuine knowledge of the human individual, the infinite qualities that theologians over the centuries have in their despair at the failings of humanity attributed to God. The task Hegel set himself was exploration of the truth of human spirit; the plumbing of the depths of an individual's soul. There is more to wonder at in the conflicted mind of a criminal, he contends, than in the starry workings of heaven and the universe. "The highest, most concentrated point," Hegel declares at the conclusion of *Logic*, "is the *pure personality*, which solely through the absolute dialectic which is its nature, no less *embraces and holds everything within itself*, because it makes itself the supremely free–the simplicity which is the first immediacy and universality." The key to the Hegelian endeavour lies in the "shadowy realm" of the categories, "the world of simple essentialities freed from all sensuous consciousness." If social science is to make the new beginning Innis pleaded for thirty years ago, the time for logic, "the absolute culture and discipline of consciousness,"[27] is surely upon us.

NOTES

1. Harold A. Innis, "A Plea for Time," pp. 61-91 in *The Bias of Communication* (Toronto: University of Toronto Press, 1951), pp. 85-86.
2. G. W. F. Hegel, *Science of Logic*, trans. A. V. Miller (London: Allen and Unwin, 1969), p. 25.
3. Cited in Hugh Kenner, "The Man Who Knew It All," *The New York Times Book Review* (June 30, 1985), p. 1.
4. *Capital: A Critique of Political Economy*, trans. Ben Fowkes (Harmondsworth, Middlesex, 1976), p. 338.
5. "Dialectical Analysis and Psychosocial Epistemology," pp. 103-124 in Kenneth J. Gergen and Mary M. Gergen, eds., *Historical Social Psychology* (Hillsdale, N.J.: Erlbaum, 1984), p. 122.
6. Steven Collins, "Categories, Concepts or Predicaments? Remarks on Mauss's Use of Philosophical Terminology," pp. 46-82 in Michael Carrithers, Steven Collins, Steven Lukes, *The Category of the Person: Anthropology, Philosophy, History* (Cambridge: Cambridge University Press, 1985), p. 46.
7. Cited in Collins, "Categories, Concepts or Predicaments?" p. 53.
8. On Kant and Durkheim see Collins, "Categories, Concepts or Predicaments?"; on Durkheim and Hegel, see Peter Knapp, "The Question of Hegelian Influence upon Durkheim's Sociology," *Sociological Inquiry* 55 (Winter 1985), pp. 1-15.
9. *Conjectures and Refutations: The Growth of Scientific Knowledge* (London: Routledge, 1963), p. 191.
10. *Science of Logic*, p. 26.
11. G. W. F. Hegel, *Logic: Being Part One of the Encyclopaedia of the Philosophical Sciences (1830)*, trans. William Wallace (Oxford: Clarendon, 1975), para. 60, *Zusätze*, p. 94.
12. "The logic of Hegel's *Logic*," pp. 85-109, in Michael Inwood, ed., *Hegel* (Oxford: Clarendon, 1985), p. 109.
13. *Logic*, paras. 13, 25, pp. 13, 45.
14. "The Indispensability of Political Theory," pp. 17-34 in David Miller and Larry Siedentop, eds., *The Nature of Political Theory* (Oxford: Clarendon, 1983), p. 17.
15. trans. J. B. Baillie (New York, 1967), p. 276.
16. *The Philosophy of Mind: Being Part Three of the Encyclopaedia of the Philosophical Sciences (1830)*, trans. William Wallace and A. V. Miller (Oxford: Clarendon, 1969), para. 43, p. 93.
17. *Philosophy of Right* (Oxford: Clarendon, 1952), para. 108, p. 76.
18. *Logic*, para. 15, p. 20.
19. *Logic*, para. 13, p. 18.
20. *Capital*, p. 532.
21. For an excellent discussion of standard accounts of profit in the economic literature see David P. Ellerman, "On the Labor Theory of Property," in *The Philosophical Forum* 16 (Summer 1985), pp. 293-326.
22. *Ibid.*, p. 744.
23. Robert Kuttner, "The Povery of Economics," *The Atlantic Monthly* (February 1985), p. 78.
24. A thorough review of this debate appears in Ralph Miliband, "State Power and Class Interests," *New Left Review* (No. 138, March-April, 1983), pp. 57-68.
25. *Logic*, paras. 196, 199, pp. 264-5.

26. *Ibid.*, p. 774.
27. *Ibid.*, pp. 841, 58.

Part II

MORAL ENGAGEMENT

3

A TYPOLOGY OF INTELLECTUALS

Christopher Lasch

1

There are several ways of thinking about the public role of a learned class, and it is useful to recognize the differences among them, even though these differences reveal themselves more clearly as ideal types than as part of an empirical historical record. Speaking very abstractly, and thinking of the term intellectual in its broadest sense, we can identify three conceptions of intellectual life in its social or public dimension. The first regards the intellectual as the voice of conscience; the second, as the voice of reason; and the third, as the voice of the imagination.

The first conception has religious roots; it is institutionalized in the church, which upholds the ideal of a disinterested love of being against the claims of self-serving worldly moralities. But this moral understanding of the intellectual's calling has also found expression in modern humanism. It is the tradition that Julien Benda accused intellectuals of betraying in *La Trahison des Clercs*. It is the tradition that Jacques Ellul defends and seeks to revive in *The Betrayal of the West* (*Trahison de l'Occident*, a deliberate allusion to Benda), in which he argues that the West's distinctive gift to the world is a "bad conscience, the habit of reflecting on itself and challenging itself."

The moral and religious ideal of the intellectual vocation makes the intellectual an adversary of the rich and powerful. In opposing the claims of wealth and power, however, the moralist does not simply align himself with the downtrodden and dispossessed in a struggle against authority. Instead, he invokes the counter-authority of tradition, which he construes, however, not as a body of timeless commandments to be unthinkingly and ritualistically obeyed but as a conversation with the past in the course of which we come to see the past with new eyes but also allow our own ideas and judgments to be changed by the past. I speak of the ideal situation, in both senses of the term. In practice, of course, the religious conception of learning hardens all too easily into a lifeless traditionalism; hence the repeated attempt to reinvigorate religion by means of the reminder that its heart is not the law but grace, contrition, and forgiveness.

It was the rigidification of religious authority, together with its unholy alliance with absolute monarchy, that helped to precipitate a new conception of intellectual life during the Enlightenment. The Enlightenment upheld reason as the antithesis of tradition. It set out to replace appeals to authority with an appeal, not to conscience, nor even to logic, but to the new standard of scientific inquiry announced by Descartes, Bacon, and Locke. Whereas the older tradition, even in its secular forms, kept alive a sense of the sacred, of mysteries not fully accessible to human intelligence, the Enlightenment waged a relentless war against "superstition" and insisted that reason can unlock the ultimate secrets of the universe. The Enlightenment tradition makes the intellectual a demystifier, debunker, and muckraker, who tears away the veil of convention and exposes life as it is, without illusions or wishful thinking. The scientific intellectual uses the voice of reason to put an end to the conspiracy of silence surrounding the dirty secrets of sex, money, and power. By reducing even the most exalted activities to the commonplace determinant of self-interest, he hopes to dispel the fears that give an aura of mystery and enchantment to political power, to love and death, and to art and dreams and day-dreams. The promise of a disenchanted world appears enabling and therapeutic, dissolving the crippling fear of the unknown.

The emancipated intellectual can identify himself with a variety of social projects and assume a variety of public roles. In the interests of simplicity, I shall distinguish two broad sub-types, the insider and the outsider. When he assumes the first of these roles, the intellectual becomes a member of the establishment, an adviser to power, a consultant, an expert, a technician, a professional problem solver, in short a mandarin, in the most general sense of the term. When he assumes the second role, he identifies himself with a counter-establishment, often conceived as a revolutionary vanguard that speaks for the oppressed and attempts to lead them to power.

It is not easy to distinguish the revolutionary intellectual from our third general type–the intellectual as alien, rebel, and renegade–except by emphasizing what the revolutionary has in common with the social technician. Both see knowledge in much the same way, as a body of morally neutral facts and theories, based on scientific methods and procedures or at least on methods and procedures derived from the natural sciences, which can be applied to the solution of social problems. The difference between the establishment and the counter-establishment intellectual is simply that the latter puts his knowledge, his understanding of history and social relations, at the service of workers and peasants, say, whereas the establishment intellectual puts it at the service of the state. The revolutionary sets himself up as an adviser not to the dominant classes but to the classes that hope to take their place. The third kind of intellectual, on the other hand, has no ambition to assume power either under the existing regime or in some revolutionary government erected on its ruins. If he identifies himself with the powerless–and our analysis so far suggests that this identification with the powerless is a frequently occurring characteristic of intellectuals in general–it is not because he hopes to lead them to power but because the experience of society's victims and outcasts appears to provide a point of view from which to criticize the prevailing customs. In his suspicion of any form of power, even when it claims to speak for the dispossessed, the rebellious or alienated intellectual is closer to the first type, the moralist, than to the man of science; but the model that appeals to him most is that modern culture-hero, the artist. Think of the difference between Marx and Bakunin, or again between Marx and Herzen. The adversary culture of the modernist intellectual is based neither on ethical tradition nor on scientific reason but on the transforming power of the imagination. The alienated intellectual's interest in the dispossessed reflects the historic alliance between bohemia and the underworld. In the sixties, the romantic rebels of the new left had little use for the working class, historically the basis of revolutionary socialism (at least in theory); instead they glorified blacks and third-world minorities, whom they saw as cultural outlaws and aliens like themselves, not as the basis of a new revolutionary order.

2

The career of C. Wright Mills exemplifies all three of these positions. Mills found himself unable to choose among competing definitions of the intellectual vocation or even, perhaps, to see very clearly how they differed from each other. Mills's thought notoriously resists classification. He was something of a Marxist, something of a populist, maybe even something of a liberal. He was a sociologist whose work was never accepted by sociologists. Yet although his work has remained anathema to most of his professional colleagues, it was nevertheless too deeply rooted in the sociological tradition, too heavily committed to the restoration of a community of shared values and common public discourse, to be acceptable to old-line Marxists. Mills's independence of conventional categories, both political and academic, was the source of both his strengths and his weaknesses.

Insofar as he defined himself as a maverick, an interloper from the heartlands, a loner who resisted institutional affiliation, Mills gravitated toward the romantic or bohemian model of the intellectual calling, though his bohemianism had a decidedly rustic flavour. No one could have accused Mills of being an aesthete. Still, he inclined to an essentially aesthetic conception of sociology, thinking of his books as "sociological poems" that would give shape to the inchoate longings of the American soul. The sprawling body of his collected works, panoramic in their attempt to squeeze the continental scope and diversity of America between covers, vaguely recalls novelists like Thomas Wolfe and Dos Passos or a later example of this type like Jack Kerouac, in all of whom, moreover, we see the same ambivalence about America, on the one hand a rejection of small-town America, on the other hand a desire to give its inarticulate struggles some kind of form and direction.

It was Mills the rebel, the James Dean of left-wing sociology, who appealed to the new left and became a new-left legend: the iconoclast, the motorcyclist, the Wobbly, the admirer of Castro. But Mills was also a Marxist of sorts, if not in the substance of his work at least in its aspiration to provide the American left with a disciplined and systematic analysis of society that would uncover law-like regularities hidden beneath the apparent flux and chaos of history. It is suggestive of this side of Mills's career that he worried so much about the "problem of the historic agency of change," which he identified, in his "Letter to the New Left," as the "most important issue of political reflection...in our time." His attempt to identify a historical successor to the working class indicates that Mills did not find entirely satisfying the role of rebel and iconoclast. He wanted to put intellectual work at the service of historical change, to identify the social groups with an interest in radical politics, and to encourage them to become conscious of their historical mission, or at least of their collective self-interest. In other words, he wanted to become not simply a sociological satirist but a counter-establishment intellectual in the tradition of Lenin and Rosa Luxembourg, whose writings he recommended to the new left in his famous letter, along with those of Marx himself.

Since he believed that the working class was finished as a revolutionary force and had no patience with the "labour metaphysic" bequeathed to the left by Victorian Marxism, Mills turned to the intellectuals themselves as the successor, or something like it, to Marx's proletariat. I quote again from the "Letter to the New Left" :

> Who is it that is getting fed up? Who is it that is getting disgusted with what Marx called 'all the old crap'? Who is it that is thinking and acting in radical ways? All over the world—in the [Soviet] bloc, outside the bloc and in between—the answer's the same: it is the young intelligentsia.

Mills never pursued these thoughts very systematically, any more than he pursued anything else very systematically, which is probably just as well in this case, since these suggestions seem to point in the direction of a theory of intellectuals as a new class, destined to overthrow the old order and to inaugurate a new reign of reason. New class theories represent the most seductive and pernicious version of the Enlightenment model of the intellectual as the voice of reason—pernicious just because it has such understandable appeal to intellectuals and to their desire to change the world instead of merely interpreting it. Mills never went this far himself, I say, and he would have been repelled by the idea that society ought to be governed by a party of intellectuals in possession of the laws of history. He did, however, attempt to work out an analogy between workers and intellectuals, the implication of which seems to be that intellectuals might play something of the same part in history that socialists once assigned to the workers. In *White Collar*, he argued that the mass production of culture eliminates intellectual craftsmanship and proletarianizes the thinking class. The "rationalization" of intellectual production generates factory-like conditions in which the intellectual "becomes the hired man of an information industry," loses control of his work, finds himself victimized by a "general speed-up," and faces the prospect of large-scale unemployment. These observations appear in a chapter bearing the evocative title, "Brains, Inc." It would be easy to draw the conclusion that the knowledge industry nurtures a new revolutionary class in the form of an embittered intellectual proletariat. Indeed some such conclusion becomes almost unavoidable when Mills insists on discussing the cultural apparatus and the "young intelligentsia" in connection with the "most important issue of political reflection in our time," the issue of a successor to the no longer revolutionary working class.

There is another and quite different reason, however, to interest ourselves in the political implications of intellectual work and the social conditions in which it is carried on. Mills spoke repeatedly of the need for intellectuals to reach a wider public. He looked forward to a "rehabilitation of publics," emphasized the contrast between publics and masses, and saw intellectual work as part of an attempt to revive the "primary publics" characteristic of a "simpler democratic society." From this point of view, the significance of the modern organization of knowledge is not that it reduces intellectuals to proletarian status but that it turns them into experts and specialists and thus cuts them off from any kind of public discourse. The concept of a public points to a definition of the intellectual very different from the definitions that make intellectuals either servants of power, servants of a powerless proletariat seeking to become a new ruling class, or simply spokesmen for the disenfranchised. When intellectuals address a public, they may still speak for the dispossessed, but they no longer seek merely to challenge complacency or to convict their readers of apathy or callous neglect. Instead of using the plight of the dispossessed to distance themselves from their readers or to proclaim their own moral superiority, they now seek, on the contrary, to reawaken the sense of common ties, the ties of humanity itself, that link the lowest and highest and thereby chasten the pride of wealth and rank. When intellectuals advance the moral claims of the lowly in this public context, it is not because the lowly are victims but because they are brothers. As brothers, they remind us that no one is self-sufficient, not even the rich man who tries to buy the illusion of absolute independence. This challenge to self-sufficiency is more radical in its implications than the usual appeal to liberal guilt, because it forces us to acknowledge how much of our social life rests not simply on exploitation or injustice but on the attempt to deny our helplessness and dependence and thus to deny any need for others. Our social life is deeply antisocial, based on a repudiation of the religious and cultural traditions that teach man to see his brothers as his principal support against the insecurities of life. The idea of the public keeps alive an attenuated memory of those traditions, a reminder that a community is more than a collection of individuals bound together by common interests or even by common values. The idea of the public reminds us that community life has a moral and educative dimension and cannot be understood merely as a means of satisfying private wants. If "man's first desire is to deny his finitude," as Wilson Carey McWilliams puts it in his splendid book on fraternity, then community life provides a corrective lesson in limits.

To read so much brotherhood into the idea of the public, it may be objected, is to read far too much into Mills's vague allusions to the subject and to carry his thought, once again, to conclusions he would have opposed. As Miller tells us, fraternity was the French revolutionary ideal that Mills (like so many others) found it most difficult to appreciate. This is probably why his thinking about publics remained undeveloped. The mere fact that he raised the subject at all, however, indicates that Mills retained some of the original sense of the intellectual's calling–the intellectual as moral teacher. Like fraternity, this is a conception that is hard for us to grasp, not least because it is so easily assimilated to the current demand, one of which we are rightly suspicious, for the humanities to play a larger part in the delineation of our so-called national purpose. Mills never had any patience at all with this kind of talk. But neither did he have much patience with the cynicism that dismisses public debate as a charade, insists that important issues are always settled by force, and demands that intellectuals choose sides in the coming class war. "The absence of publicly relevant mind," he wrote in *The Power Elite*, "has come to mean that powerful decisions and important policies are not made in such a way as to be justified or attacked; in short, debated in any intellectual form." Here is the basis of a salutary appeal to intellectuals to concern themselves with the old-fashioned business of moral and political education, not with the deployment of expertise, with the leadership of would-be revolutionary movements or new classes, or with the celebration of the moral superiority of the underdog.

3

Mills wavered, then, between three competing conceptions of the intellectual's calling, speaking sometimes as a romantic rebel and outsider, sometimes as an adviser to the rising new left, and sometimes as a moralist or public philosopher appealing to the public conscience and seeking to revive a lost tradition of moral discourse. Something of the same thing can be said of Freud and of the psychoanalytic movement in general. Psychoanalysis can be viewed as a science, as a continuation of the romantic critique of the Enlightenment, or as a contribution to moral philosophy. Freud himself saw psychoanalysis as a science, but he used the term so broadly, at times, as to imply that the psychoanalytic practitioner has more in common with a philosopher or preacher than with a technician in a white coat. He defended lay analysis and resisted the medicalization of psychoanalytic practice. The battle over this issue, eventually won by those who advocated medical training as the basis of psychoanalytic preparation, registered the conflicting tendencies within the psychoanalytic movement. Freud objected to the "obvious American tendency to turn psycho-analysis into a mere housemaid of psychiatry." Not only did he not think that medical training should be required of analysts, he went so far as to discourage it. In his view, analysts ought to be trained not only in the rudiments of anatomy and physiology but in mythology, the psychology of religion, and the classics of literature. Moreover, he insisted that personal experience of suffering and the capacity for introspection represented the indispensable foundation of psychoanalytic understanding. Ernest Jones, who did not agree with Freud's position but was close enough to be able to understand it, noted that the "basic fact" of psychoanalytic training was the discovery that "no motive has been discovered...making possible the investigation of the deepest layers of the mind other than that of personal *suffering*." But although Jones found Freud's opinions "extraordinarily interesting," he himself believed that psychoanalysis would have to become a branch of medicine, if only to weed out the "wild analysts" who discredited the profession by practicing without a license. This was the position adopted by the psychoanalytic movement as a whole, after the movement's center of gravity shifted from Europe to the United States.

In opposition to the medicalization of psychoanalysis, a few mavericks and rebels sought to ally psychoanalysis not with medical science but with the romantic criticism of society. Robert Lindner, himself a lay analyst and social critic, attributed the "relative stagnation" of psycho-analysis in the forties and fifties "almost exclusively to the insistence upon the prerequisite of a medical education for a license to practice.... In the place of broad systemized knowledge of man, his culture and his works, this majority [of medical practitioners] possesses a handful of clin-ical facts wrapped about with terminological vagaries." Like Herbert Marcuse, Lindner accused post-Freudian psychoanalysis of celebrating conformity and adjustment, whereas it ought to side, he thought, with the rebel and social outcast. With good reason, Russell Jacoby compares Lindner to C. Wright Mills. His books, which include *Rebel without a Cause* (1944) and *Prescription for Rebellion* (1952), upheld a rebellious atti-tude against the new social ethic demanded by a society of organization men. "Today," Lindner wrote, "in the struggle between man and Society over the issue of conformity, Society is winning."

A third view of psychoanalysis attempts to revive a half-forgotten tradition of moral and public discourse in which the intellectual addresses his appeal to conscience, not to scientific reason on the one hand or to the romantic dream of liberation on the other. From this point of view, the value of psychoanalysis lies in its capacity to recapture some of the deepest insights of an earlier religious tradition. I do not mean that it vindicates the rights of personhood or asserts the dignity of the individual, as humanistic psychology would have it—nothing as nebu-lous and uplifting as that. I mean that it helps to recover the spiritual dimension of evil, if I can put it that way. It helps to distinguish instinct from desires, the biological will to survive from the psychological urge to deny our limitations either by making ourselves lords over nature or by achieving a blissful reunion with nature. What Freud called narcissism expresses some of what is expressed in another tradition by the concepts of pride and envy. Narcissism longs for the absence of longing, a condi-tion of absolute peace. It seeks to free itself from the prison of the body, not because it seeks death—though it can lead people to commit suicide—but because it has no conception of death and regards the bodily ego as a lower form of life, besieged by the clamorous demands of the flesh. It follows a "backward path" to a lost paradise, but it can also become the basis of a mature idealism so exalted that it will sacrifice bodily comfort for a cause, even life itself, preferring death to dishonour.

It was Melanie Klein, I believe, who first set out on the path of inquiry that has led to a new understanding of separation anxiety and its role in the development of the ego ideal and in the psychology of narcis-sism. The titles of her leading essays testify to Klein's ability to moralize Freud's concepts without any loss of analytical rigour: "Love, Guilt, and Reparation," "Envy and Gratitude," "The Early Development of Conscience in the Child." In the last of these essays—the first (1934) in point of composition—she distinguished between the "sadistic nucleus of the super-ego" and the feelings of pity that arouse "less anxiety and more sense of guilt." In "Love, Guilt, and Reparation," written three years later, she worked out this idea more fully, arguing that conscience, as distinguished from the primitive superego, rests on feelings of gratitude. The superego, on the other hand, rests on the fear of retaliation–that is, on the projection of one's own destructive urges outward, in the first instance against the figure of the punitive and persecuting mother, and later against the father. Conscience is quite different; it originates in the impulse to make amends. In the same essay, Klein proposes a marvellously resonant distinction between exploration and conquest, conflicting attitudes toward nature that can be traced back to the infant's conflicting emotions about its mother. She speculates that the exploratory urge–the search for the promised land of milk and honey–rests not only on aggressive drives but on the need to make reparation to the mother, "to put back into his mother the good things [the child] had robbed her of in phantasy." In exploration–which "need not be expressed in an actual physical exploration of the world, but may extend to other fields, for instance, to any kind of scientific discovery" or again, to artistic creation–the wish for reunion with the mother no longer seeks the shortest path (greedy incorporation of the mother) but proceeds from the wish to make amends. And since "the relation to nature which arouses such strong feelings of love, appreciation, admiration and devotion has much in common with the relations to one's mother, as has long been recognized by poets," the "struggle with nature"–insofar as the exploratory impulse prevails over the spirit of conquest and subjugation–"is therefore partly felt to be a struggle to *preserve nature*, because it expresses also the wish to make reparation to her (mother)."

In "Envy and Gratitude," as well as in her very late essay, "Some Reflections on the Oresteia," Klein examined the relations between envy and greed. She pointed out that greed is an "impetuous and insatiable craving, exceeding what the subject needs and what the object is able and willing to give." Drawing not only on clinical experience but on literature and theology, she showed that envy has always been thought of, quite appropriately, as a disposition to destroy the object of insatiable craving, to bite the hand that feeds you, and as an emotion, moreover, that intensifies the craving behind it at the same time that it destroys the capacity for enjoyment. Klein found the origins of these feelings in the infant's fear of separation. The child needs not only the mother's nourishment but the unconditional, enveloping security with which it is associated. It is because the biological need for nourishment is suffused with desire that the infant's greed is insatiable; even the temporary absence of the mother gives rise to frustration and to feelings of rage. According to Klein, the young child envies the mother's power to give and withhold life and projects this resentment in the form of threatening figures, images of the "child's own hate, increased by being in the parents' power." But the attempt to restore a euphoric sense of well-being by splitting images associated with frustration from gratifying images arouses painful fears of persecution and, indeed, even spoils the capacity for pleasure and enjoyment. "Greed, envy, and persecutory anxiety, which are bound up with each other, inevitably increase each other." It is not for nothing that envy ranks among the seven deadly sins. Klein goes so far as to suggest that it is unconsciously felt to be the greatest sin of all, because it "spoils and harms the good object which is the source of life." The associations between envy and the fear of retaliation are expressed in the Greek concept of *hubris*, usually translated as pride but better understood as a form of envy and greed, rooted in the infant's total dependence on its caretakers and its overwhelming need for the warmth and nourishment they provide. Quoting Gilbert Murray, Klein points out that "*hubris* grasps at more, bursts bounds and breaks the order: it is followed by *Dike*, Justice, which reestablishes them." The Greek idea of justice, which punishes *hubris*, expresses more or less what is expressed by the psychoanalytic concept of the superego. The superego represents the fear of retaliation, called up by powerful impulses to destroy the very source of life. Guilt, on the other hand, as opposed to the fear of persecution, derives from a "feeling of gratitude for goodness received," from the "ability to accept and assimilate the loved primal object (not only as a source of good) without greed and envy." This attitude, I might add, also goes by the name of grace.

Psychoanalysis can be understood not merely as a new science or as a critique of a repressive civilization but as a critique of human pretensions, which incorporates ancient cultural traditions and gives them a new basis in clinical observation. Considered from the last of these perspectives, it has much to contribute to a revival of public philosophy. Indeed it might serve as the very basis of such a philosophy, which has to rest on an acknowledgment of our dependent position in the world, of the limits of human knowledge, and of our need for others who nevertheless remain separate from ourselves. It is the discovery of human limits that creates the possibility of fraternity; and it is the refusal to acknowledge those limits, in the last analysis, that makes the idea of fraternity so difficult for a modern emancipated intellectual (like C. Wright Mills) to fathom.

NOTE

Parts of this essay were published earlier as commentaries in *Salmagundi* (Nos. 70-71, Spring-Summer, 1986), a special issue on intellectuals.

4

HUMANIST SOCIOLOGY: SCIENTIFIC AND CRITICAL

Gregory Baum

1

When I began my studies in sociology at the New School, after having taught theology for many years, I was greatly impressed by the sociological critique of positivism. The writings of Max Scheler and Karl Mannheim were my guides at the time.[1] While their sociological and political views differed considerably, they were united in their lament over the effort to assimilate the social sciences to the natural sciences. They objected to a sociology that understood itself as a scientific enterprise to explain social action by discovering the laws operative in collective human behaviour. They were critical of the claim that sociology was value-free and objective. They regarded this as an illusion. Each of them in his own way developed a sociology of knowledge which showed that the knowledge of the social reality involved the knowing subject, and that this knowledge was affected by the subject's social location and value orientation. Scheler and Mannheim had respect for the scientific method. But if sociology restricted itself to this method it had to reduce the complex human reality to measurable categories and thus confine itself to examining the external aspect of social action. In particular, positivistic social science had to abstract from the interior dimension of human existence.

Positivistic social science has a reductionist impact on modern culture. Positivism persuades people that the only reliable truth is scientifically demonstrated truth, that values are soft, and that ethics is a purely private affair. Science and technology here easily become the metaphor of human existence. People begin to conceive of themselves as part of a system that operates according to fixed, impersonal laws. In this understanding society is neither an organic given held together by shared values (as Scheler supposed, in line with the conservative tradition), nor a social project in which people are creatively involved (as Mannheim supposed, following the liberal tradition). Both sociologists were convinced that, in excluding ethics from public life and public policy debates, positivism had dangerous cultural consequences.

They were also concerned about its political consequences. For as the investigating subject in the natural sciences is superior to the object under study and entitled to manipulate and if need be, destroy the object, so will positivistically inclined social scientists regard themselves superior to the object of their studies, i.e. human beings acting in society, and be tempted to manipulate them and engineer their future. Human beings here count less and less. Positivism appears here as an ideology that fosters domination.

From the beginning of my studies, then, I was convinced that sociology must be humanistic, take into account the entire human being, respect persons in society. I was therefore pleased to learn from Max Weber that social action, the object of sociology, was constituted by two dimensions, behaviour and meaning, the one external and measurable, the other internal and not measurable, but understandable through appropriate interpretation. Sociological science is both scientific and hermeneutic.[2]

Max Weber's formulation prevented me from going overboard in my reaction to positivism. As a theologian I had my own reasons for being unhappy with positivistic social science. Many sociological studies of religion looked upon religion simply from the outside, in terms of religious behaviour, without a serious effort to understand the meaning this behaviour had to believers and the believing community. Religious people are often offended by positivistic studies of religion because they do not recognize themselves in these studies.

At the same time, I met theologians engaged in sociological studies who were grateful to positivistic scholarship because it delivered them from legends regarding the Church and the history of Christianity with which they had been brought up and which they later in life found difficult to swallow. Positivism was liberating at some moments in history. Mannheim acknowledged that in certain historical situations, false and socially dangerous ideas promoted by those in power were exploded by the application of the scientific method. Thus positivistic research has invalidated various theories that tried to divide humanity into superior and inferior races. However much one argues against positivism, it is important not to reject empirical, quantitative research. Humanistic sociology must remain scientific.

The positivism which Scheler and Mannheim castigated was not simply a scientific and philosophical theory, but also an intellectual atmosphere at the university and a mood of modern civilization. Many social scientists who do not regard themselves as positivists in the technical sense engage in sociological research out of a set of practical presuppositions that are in fact positivistic. They understand sociological research as objective, value-free, and demonstrable by the scientific method. And vast numbers of people in society who have never heard of positivism believe that the problems in society can be analysed objectively by social science and solved by the appropriate office through the implementation of a valuefree, scientifically demonstrated policy. Social problems can be solved, people think, without reference to values, without ethical reflection, without wisdom and virtue.

Criticism of positivism has led some thinkers to the repudiation of the scientific dimension of sociology altogether. When I began my studies in sociology, I read the works of Alfred Schutz, who brought phenomenological sociology to North America.[3] He exerted considerable influence on the discipline. A particular reading of Max Weber led Schutz to the idea that the social reality was created by the meaning which people assigned to their actions, the shared meaning through which they constituted their common world, and that for this reason it was in the language of everyday life that these meanings were negotiated and established. To gain an understanding of society we must investigate our daily consciousness of acting with others in the creation of the life world. We must unpack the implicit and unthematized knowledge contained in the language of every day. The life world is the primary world to which we belong: the more specialized studies of this world, for instance in sociology, are derived from this life world and never transcend it. Sociological research constitutes a special subworld in the primary world constituted by people through shared meaning. This approach reduces the scientific status of sociology if it does not cancel it altogether. Sociology is here mainly concerned with the analysis of consciousness and the roles which people play in the world constituted by them. The influence of Alfred Schutz is found in Peter Berger's sociology, which presents itself as anti-positivist and humanistic.[4] Schutz's influence is also found in ethnomethodology.

There are other social thinkers who repudiate the scientific character of sociology. Some reject altogether the modern project, defined by the Enlightenment. According to them it was a grave error to conceive of human reason as an instrument of human liberation, to promote science, technology, and control of nature, and to struggle for a more rational, scientific, and responsible society. This sort of romantic reaction is found in some philosophers. I am more familiar with religious thinkers who repudiate the modern project. Both Neo-Thomism in Catholicism and Neo-Orthodoxy in Protestantism can be read in this way. The most influential contemporary theologian who defends this approach is the important French Protestant, Jacques Ellul, who argues that the Enlightenment project is dehumanizing. Science and technology have transformed the human milieu into a machine, a technological society, in which even the best efforts at reform promote the manipulation of people, their subordination to technical ends, and the systematic distortion of public communication.[5] Making use of Max Weber's concept of "rationalization" and "disenchantment of the world," Jacques Ellul argues that "la technique," the dominant model orienting truth and values in modern society, inevitably produces a dehumanizing culture. Technology is so powerful that no force can stand against it: there is hope only for individuals who stand apart from it, who step into the margin, who refuse to play the game. Christians are called to stand apart.

Ellul has had considerable influence on certain Canadian thinkers, among them George Grant and Douglas Hall.[6] While Ellul is a dedicated, thoughtful Christian who deserves great respect, it is my impression that he vulgarizes the sociology of Max Weber. Apart from certain polemical passages in which Weber expressed his fear of the future, the German sociologist used his categories, including "rationalization," as ideal types, as paradigms, to observe how far certain trends have gone in society. Weber's categories including "rationalization" pointed to currents in society; they did not offer a conceptual account of society. Weber never denied that dominant structures and trends were opposed by countervailing movements in the same society. But by making Weber's ideal type the conceptual image of modern society, Ellul renders counter trends in society invisible and hence leaves no room for explaining the purpose of his own publishing activity. For if in technological society all communication is transformed into propaganda, then this would also apply to his own books, printed, published and distributed by technique. Despite my respect for Ellul's spiritual stance, I feel that he offers the reader bad sociology.

2

I oppose the effort to defend the humanistic character of sociology by excluding quantitative research and the scientific method altogether. There is no reason to despise hard data, measurement, and demonstration. Yet it is only to the extent that social action is behaviour that it can be quantified. The meaning dimension cannot. Meaning demands understanding. Sociology includes the task of interpretation. Weber spoke of *verstehende Soziologie*. We must interpret the meaning of the action in the social setting, determined by commonly held expectations, "the shared meaning," and we must interpret the meaning the action has to the actor, "the expressive meaning." It is this interpretative process that positivism has suppressed. Positivism looks only at behaviour: it is behaviourism.

How does the sociologist go about understanding the meaning of social action? The scientific method is not enough. What is necessary is to lay aside the cultural presuppositions of one's own class and society and enter into the thought world of those whose social action is being studied. One must enter their mental universe. What is required is empathy for the people who are being examined, accompanied by growing self-knowledge. For the interpretation of the meaning which actors assign to their action must be humanly credible to the researcher. By putting themselves in the historical situation of the groups under study, researchers explore their own self-understanding and discover new possibilities and powers within themselves. Sociological research calls not just for scientific reason but for expanded awareness, openness to new experiences, imaginative identification with others. If this analysis is correct, sociologists need more than training in methodology: they need encouragement to become educated persons, persons of culture and imagination.

Since sociology aspires to insights into human action and the life of society, it cannot rely simply on the scientific method. Scientific reason alone cannot arrive at a deep understanding of human beings. Marx, Durkheim and Weber were philosophers as well as scientists. There is no substitute for wisdom. Researchers want to remain in dialogue with the classical sociologists whose work continues to act as guide and inspiration for understanding the social reality.

Sociology is then scientific in a wider sense, including the quantitative and the qualitative, including measurement and interpretation. How can the proposals made by scientific, interpretative sociology be verified? They must stand up to critical examination of the community of scholars. Like all truths in the natural and the human sciences, they must be validated by evidence. In sociology it must be shown that the interpretation makes sense, takes into account the available data, sheds light on connected phenomena, and explains relations that were hitherto obscure. Daring proposals of interpretative sociology become acceptable if they give rise to creative approaches in other areas of inquiry. As I write this paragraph on how to demonstrate theses proposed by interpretative sociology, I inevitably think of the many ways in which Max Weber demonstrated his thesis that the affinity between the Puritan ethic and the spirit of capitalism affected the rapid spread of modernity in Europe and North America. Weber's thesis gave rise to many research projects into related areas of inquiry. He himself examined the economic ethos (*Wirtschaftsethik*) of the world religions. Many researchers after him have recognized cultural heritage as an indispensible factor in the sociology of economic development. Development proposals in third-world countries are doomed to failure if the cultural factor, the ethos of the people, is not taken seriously.[7]

For Max Weber scientific, interpretative sociology was still an objective, value-free scholarly enterprise. He emphasized the value-neutrality of social science against the German government that wanted sociologists at the university to provide arguments in support of its own policies.

Weber accepted the Kantian distinction between fact and value. He realized of course that sociological research was always carried on from a particular perspective, which in some way influenced the result. But he thought that this perspective was freely chosen by the social scientist. The social scientist chooses the question to be studied, chooses what aspects are to be examined and what aspects are to be left out. Still, once the issue and the orientation have been chosen, social science intends to be value-free and objective. The results of the inquiry must be demonstrated and stand up before the court of scholars, whatever their values and their political vision may be. Scientific rationality, Weber argued, was universal. We note, however, that Weber's distinction between fact and value differed from the similar distinction made by the positivists. For Weber the facts, the historical data, included intentionality, i.e. the subjective dimension.

While Weber defended the value-free nature of the social sciences, he wanted them to be value-relevant.[8] He thought that civic responsibility demanded that sociologists use their scientific skills to examine the impact of present social and economic policies on the population and study what would happen if these were replaced by alternative policies. What sector of society would be helped if this or that policy were adopted by the government? Would the burden on the poor increase or be relieved if this or that public measure were introduced? While sociology as a social science must abstract from ethics, it could nonetheless be helpful to those engaged in political life. Sociological research could enable politically responsible persons with an ethical vision to decide whether certain policies would actually help people and fulfil their political expectations.

When I studied Weber at the New School I was puzzled by his deterministic conclusion in regard to modern industrial society. He spoke of "the fate" of modernity. He lamented that the disenchantment of the world had become ineluctable. He predicted the end of utopia. These were polemical positions, basically at odds with his sociological approach, which presumed that society always remained open to human agency. My first essay, later published as an article, examined whether there was empirical evidence in contemporary culture (the sixties) that the world was not totally disenchanted, that utopias had not totally disappeared, that overcoming alienation was not necessarily an unrealistic dream.[9] I have always felt that Weber's deterministic-sounding judgement on modernity was part of a particular German ideological trend that associated industrialization with vulgarity and the decline of high culture.[10]

Weber's sociology was scientific and humanistic: for the significant human facts which sociology studied included subjectivity. Weber was not a determinist. Despite his lament about the inevitable fate of modernity, his sociology respected the freedom of persons as effective agents in the social process.

As a Christian theologian I had sympathy for this point of view. History remains open to human intervention. At the same time, I recognized that following Max Weber was opting for a particular sociological paradigm among several others. There were sociologists who saw individual persons and groups of persons more closely integrated into society and who therefore interpreted social action largely in reference to the function it exercises in society as a whole. Something bigger than the persons involved worked itself out through their social action. Both Marx and Durkheim understood society as a close fit, the former in a conflictual and the latter in an organic mode. Both understood social action as an expression of major forces operative in society as a whole. Max Weber did not believe in totalities. For him society was not a close fit. It was not held together by the harsh bonds of exploiter/exploited relationships legitimated by an all-pervasive ideology, nor was it held together by shared values, shared vision, shared symbols and rituals. For Weber the nation state was not a close weave. What held modern society together was largely the power (*Herrschaft*) of government to make people conform to law and order. Weber took seriously the exploiter/exploited relationships in society, and not only in the sphere of economics; he took seriously as well the various forms of cultural legitimation that defended the existing order. But he did not think that this domination produced a closed system: for him there remained room for countervailing trends sparked by the enterprise of imaginative individuals and promoted by movements inspired by them. Weber entertained a pluralist understanding of society.

Students of sociology learn very quickly that they must choose among several sociological paradigms. Should they follow the functionalist approach, a Marxian conflict sociology, Weberian pluralism, or symbolic interactionism? How do sociologists choose? The choice is first of all a scientific task: sociologists want to choose the paradigm that is able to take into account all the data, that remains open to new research and discoveries, that proposes causal relations that seem credible in the situation, and that has been used successfully in important scientific studies by other sociologists, especially by sociologists one admires. But the choice of a paradigm is not purely an exercise in scientific rationality. It has a philosophical dimension. All sociological theory has implicit in it a philosophy of human life. Researchers turn to a particular school of sociology because they have an intellectual affinity with it, approve of its implicit philosophy, or less reflectively, because it corresponds to society's self-understanding mediated by mainstream culture. The choice of a paradigm is not value-free.

3

Weber's understanding of value-free social science thus became increasingly difficult for me to accept. I realized of course that Weber's emphasis was a corrective. He wanted to protect scholars from government pressure and to shield sociology from ideological invasions. Thus he was critical of doctrinaire Marxist sociology which approached scientific research with an antecedently determined concept of infrastructure and superstructure, where the latter was wholly determined by the former. But should it not be possible to protect sociology from ideological distortions without claiming value-neutrality? Why should sociology not become more explicit about the value-assumptions operative within it?

In my studies at the New School it was not Marx but Ernst Troeltsch who made me go beyond Weber. For Troeltsch social science was humanistic and critical. In an essay I wrote while at the New School, later published as an article, I examined Troeltsch's understanding of engaged scholarship.[11] Historical and sociological science cannot be separated from evaluation.

Troeltsch rejected the Kantian distinction between fact and value. He rejected as well the hidden presupposition of this distinction, namely the radical separation of subject and object. For Troeltsch the subject, the researcher, was not a human mind, identical to all other human minds, equipped with a cognitive apparatus ready to encounter the world. The researcher's mind had been constituted by a history, by interaction with culture, by personal experiences and material interests. The researcher belongs to a certain world, is located in an historical context. And conversely, the social phenomenon under study, the object of research, has also been constituted by an historical development. It, too, is the result of a social process and belongs to a certain world. Troeltsch recognized that in all likelihood a relation exists between the world of the subject and the world of the object. The historical development that has produced the object has had an influence on the shaping of the researcher's mind; conversely, the world of the researcher may well have been involved in the formation of the object now being studied. The radical separation of subject and object is, therefore, an illusion. Something of the object is in the subject, and something of the subject is in the object. The same history has generated both subject and object. History and social science arrive at reliable knowledge only when the relationship between subject and object has been clarified.

Troeltsch's position is immediately convincing when we illustrate it by reference to the poor, the unemployed, the Native peoples, the victims of society. When a researcher studies social phenomena pertaining to the underclass then it would appear obvious that the world of the researcher is related to the object under study. The same history has generated subject and object. An attempt to deny this relationship, to approach the research project in an objective, value-free manner, would disguise the historical reality, perpetuate an illusion, and in an unconscious way give social science an ideological twist. In daily life we are well aware that as we walk past a distraught and depressed Canadian Indian on the street we mourn: we realize that the observer and the observed are interrelated by a common history. They, the observed, are the way they are partly because of the world with which we, the observers, are identified.

For Troeltsch, history and social science research constituted a dynamic process, a back-and-forth, a circle, as he himself called it. First the researcher examines the social phenomenon under study by relying on empirical, measurable data (behaviour) and on the hermeneutical effort to understand this other world (meaning). Here researchers abandon their cultural presuppositions as much as possible. They seek "objectivity." But then a second phase begins. By the internal dynamics of the human mind researchers are taken back to their own social world with questions that have arisen from the research. The researchers' own world begins to appear somewhat different to them. They now see certain similarities, differences, and connections between the two worlds. Even the categories in which the researchers have been taught to think become somewhat problematic to them. They discover that their mind-set has undergone a certain change. With this altered mind-set the researchers now return to the social phenomenon under study. There they will make new observations, discover aspects previously overlooked, and gain deeper insight into the world of the object. This back-and-forth will continue. Troeltsch thinks that this process aims at discovering a single perspective in which both worlds, the world of the object and the world of the subject, appear in their historical interrelation. In this process the researchers themselves will have undergone a certain transformation.

Positivistic social scientists regard the researcher's mindset as non-problematic. When research comes to conclusions that are unreliable and misleading then they suspect an error in the empirical observations or a mistake in the application of logic. They do not suspect that the subject itself could be the source of distortion.

For Troeltsch, on the other hand, the transformation in the researcher's mind deserves the greatest attention. An almost inevitable dynamic forces the mind to compare and bring together the world of the object and its own world, the world of the subject. It is almost impossible to study the prisons of a distant country, the treatment of women in a remote culture or the exercise of authority in a certain period of history, without returning with questions about how our society organizes its prisons, treats women, and exercises authority. Such critical questions can be avoided only if a special effort is made to suppress the mind's inner dynamic.

This dynamic, Troeltsch insists, has an ethical dimension. It is almost impossible for the human mind to interrupt the connection between *is* and *ought*. When we study what "is," it is almost impossible not to desire immediately what we think "ought" to be. People with different ethical visions will entertain different wishes of what ought to be. But the impulse to relate a given situation to what we think it ought to be is almost universal. Only a special effort of suppression can interrupt this dynamic of the mind. Troeltsch argues that the ethical vision of researchers, their desire for a specific future of their own world, has a research-guiding function. It affects the questions they ask, the slice of historical reality they cut out as "fact," the categories they choose to understand the social phenomenon, and the sensitivity with which they read the empirical data. More than that, the ethical engagement of researchers affects the circle, the back-and-forth, the approach to seeing the two worlds of subject and object together. History and social science, even when faithful to the scientific method, are always an intellectual exercise that promotes a certain cultural vision, a certain kind of society, a certain moral universe.

What is the ethical vision the social scientist ought to adopt? Here Troeltsch remained somewhat vague. He believed that in each society there emerges a rationally discoverable cultural ideal of greater human freedom and greater human depth that remains within the possibilities created by the past and commands social commitment in the present. Troeltsch repudiated absolute values: he thought the task of humanism was to overcome history by history. He was convinced that an appropriate cultural ideal could be worked out for European society after World War I. Troeltsch helped to formulate the problematic that was to preoccupy Max Scheler and Karl Mannheim, even if they came to divergent conclusions. But Troeltsch did not pay much attention to the Marxist insight, later so influential in many currents of political science, social philosophy and liberation theology, that what was needed was a critique of domination and an ethical commitment of human emancipation.

Ernst Troeltsch then differed from his friend and colleague Max Weber. Social science was not value-free. On the contrary, social science always operated out of a value perspective. Science and commitment went together. There are moments of objectivity when the researcher abandons his or her own world and surrenders totally to the object under study; and there are moments of subjectivity when the researcher returns to his or her own world, undergoes a certain transformation of consciousness, and approaches the object with new questions. The objective dimension, taken with utmost seriousness, protects the research from the influence of wishful thinking or propaganda, and the subjective dimension protects it from becoming an ideology promoting a scientific value-free society.

I found Troeltsch's position that social science always operates out of a value perspective fully convincing. It was validated for me every day as I studied sociological books and articles: the value-perspective of the sociologists always came through to me, even when the authors claimed to be value-free. Sociological studies inevitably have a political impact, at least in a broad sense. These studies promote an intellectual culture that makes people look at society in a certain way and entertain certain expectations in regard to it. Positivism, for instance, despite its claim of total objectivity, is not politically innocent. On the right and on the left, positivism fosters a view of society that is wholly determined by scientifically discoverable laws intrinsic to it. Positivism, on the right and on the left, overlooks creative personal agency and fails to see society as open to human initiative. The attention on structure easily makes sociologists neglect the role played by independent human endeavour. Among the classical sociologists, Weber was the one most concerned with protecting human agency and countervailing trends in society. In this Troeltsch did not disagree with his friend. In recent years the work of Anthony Giddens has provided a critical sociology that makes room for and emphasizes the ongoing relevance of personal agency.

4

Since social science inevitably operates out of certain ethical presuppositions, it would be scientifically more appropriate if sociologists laid their cards on the table, revealed their ethical vision of society, and defended their option with rational arguments. A sustained rational investigation of this kind would protect social scientists from prejudice and sentimentality. It would also introduce social science to a sustained ethical discourse. The claim of value-neutrality made by social science has removed ethics from the public debate of social policies. A humanistic, critical social science would give ethical reflection a recognized standing in social and political policy discussions.

This value-oriented understanding of social science was my point of entry into the study of the Frankfurt School. I was greatly impressed by Critical Theory's critique of domination, its analysis of the political relevance of culture, and its insistence on an emancipatory commitment in the social sciences–also by its dialectical critique of the Enlightenment. Horkheimer and Adorno persuasively argued that at the beginning the Enlightenment looked upon human reason as the organ by which men and women were meant to free themselves and become the subjects of their own history, but that now, in its present stage, the Enlightenment tradition had become an obstacle to liberation.[12] What has happened? At the beginning Enlightenment reason embraced scientific or instrumental reason as well as ethical or practical reason. Practical reason touched upon the nature and destiny of human being. Practical reason was evaluative. Yet over the last century and a half Enlightenment reason has increasingly collapsed into scientific or instrumental reason. Enlightenment culture has become increasingly concerned with means, no longer with ends. Rationality no longer includes ethical reflection. Ethical reason has disappeared from the social sciences and from the debates of public policy. The scientific world view that has emerged leaves no room for rational concern for human values and human destiny.

In reponse to this dialectic, Critical Theory does not reject the Enlightenment altogether; it is critical of the romantic option and conservative strategies to return to a pre-Enlightenment intellectual universe; instead Critical Theory seeks to overcome the one-sidedness of the Enlightenment tradition by retrieving the ethical dimension of reason. The Frankfurt School advocates a return to practical reason.

Coming to the Frankfurt School from Troeltsch and from my own theological background, I was greatly impressed by their attempt to retrieve practical reason. Many theologians have reacted favourably to Critical Theory. Yet with many of my colleagues I felt that the Frankfurt School did not take the retrieval of ethical reason seriously enough. They did not ask the question how values are generated, sustained and communicated. They tried to overcome "liberal" reason by a more solidary form of rationality, and hence retained the Enlightenment suspicion of the non-rational elements in community, ethnic heritage and religious tradition. They had few words in which to express their ethical concern and no rites and symbols to celebrate it with. A certain insensitivity to the ethical remains a characteristic of the secular left to this day, including sympathetic critics like Jurgen Habermas.

Ernst Troeltsch, possibly because of his theological background, had a much greater sense that ethical convictions were largely mediated through community experiences. This historical understanding of the origin of values was defended against the secular left by another theologian, Paul Tillich, in his book, *The Socialist Decision*, written out of a socialist commitment in 1932.[13] Tillich argues that socialism wanted to overcome the human alienation created by modern individualistic and utilitarian rationality. But because socialism tried to do this simply by applying another form of rationality, a more social form of reason and a more collective form of self-interest, it could never succeed: one cannot overcome the shortcomings of rationality simply by a new application of reason. What was required for socialist reconstruction, Tillich believed, was the rooting of the political effort in value traditions, community experiences, including religious aspirations. By themselves these traditions are dangerous guides in the political order, but if these values are strictly subordinated to justice, to equality, to universal participation, then they will make an essential contribution to the creation of a more just and more human society. Tillich here defended a point of view that has recently been adopted by liberation theology.

Through the impact of liberation theology, this point of view has been taken up in the official teaching of the Catholic Church. The following of Jesus, we are told, calls for "the preferential option for the poor."[14] This option embodies a double commitment: to look at society from the perspective of the powerless and to witness solidarity with their struggle for justice. The option has a hermeneutic and an activist dimension. Catholics are encouraged to exercise their social responsibility through this option; they are also asked to re-read and re-assimilate their religious tradition. The preferential option stands against all forms of domination and hence resembles the emancipatory commitment of Critical Theory, but because of its rootedness in religious experience, tradition and community, the preferential option also differs from this purely secular, emancipatory commitment. In line with Tillich, and following the more recent liberation theology, Catholic social teaching is worried about the social commitment to liberation that is secular in principle.

That social science and ethical commitment must go in tandem is a thesis that is controversial in most sociology departments. For what this thesis means is that sociology research carried on without an emancipatory commitment will arrive at conclusions that in one way or another strengthen the power of the dominative forces. And if sociology is practised without respect for the spiritual and its historical sources, its conclusions will contribute to the spiritual empoverishment of the present age. Here engagement precedes science, here engagement is the precondition of scientific truth. And here the cultural and political impact of sociological research is one of the norms by which its truth is validated.

What are the arguments given in this paper that sociological research understood in this fashion is not propaganda nor an exercise in ideology? I have been critical of positivism and pleaded for a humanistic sociology. At the same time, I have defended the scientific character of sociology. One of the norms of verification remains the scientific method applied to quantitative data. This scientific character protects the entire exercise from becoming wishful thinking or propaganda. Secondly I have emphasized the hermeneutical task of sociology. Here the researcher takes seriously the object under investigation, listens to the people whose social action is being studied, abandons preconceived notions, and interprets what the social action means to the actors. This process protects the humanistic dimension of sociology. The sociologists refuse to analyze social action by turning at once to causes hidden in social structures, causes that produce their historical effects totally behind the backs of the actors. To prepare themselves for the hermeneutic task researchers want to remain in dialogue with the classical sociological texts. But then there is the third, the critical, evaluative dimension. It is often difficult for researchers to decide when to turn from the hermeneutic to the analytical task. But when the sociologist does search for causes, he or she must choose a particular paradigm around which the data are assembled and in the light of which proposals for possible causes are made. I have argued that the choice of a paradigm has value-implications. It defines an approach to society that is inevitably value-laden. It should be added that the paradigm used in the analysis is simply what Weber calls an ideal type. This means that for each case it is necessary to justify why it is appropriate to use this ideal type and not another. If the paradigm is absolutized, if it is accorded universal validity, then social science is in danger of moving into ideology. But critical reflection on the paradigm can overcome this danger. For all these reasons, it is no contradiction to affirm the scientific character of sociology and at the same time insist that it is value-based and value-oriented.

5

By way of conclusion allow me to summarize my argument. I have repudiated positivistic social science and called for a humanistic sociology. Yet I did not favour all sociological approaches that called themselves humanistic. I rejected various attempts to discredit empirical research and the scientific method in sociology. In my eyes phenomenological sociology does not do justice to the scientific dimension. I expressed great sympathy for Max Weber's *verstehende Soziologie* because it embraced both the quantitative and the hermeneutic method in sociology. What made me uncomfortable was Weber's claim that sociological research intended to be value-free and objective. This claim seemed to be contradicted by the daily experience of students of sociology who discover a value-orientation in every sociological text they read. Humanistic sociology, I concluded, has an evaluative dimension. I favour a sociology that aims at justice, fosters emancipation, and promotes humanity. Sociology should be a critical intellectual enterprise, critical of the object and critical of the subject. It should uncover the structures and attitudes of domination in the object and bring to consciousness the subjectivity of the community of researchers. Sociology is grounded in values and in turn promotes values. Science and commitment go hand in hand. While I have great sympathy for Critical Theory, I feel that its retrieval of the ethical dimension is too unhistorical, too rational, too indifferent to the religious sources of the human quest for value and meaning. I am persuaded therefore that a humanistic sociology that is both scientific and emancipatory remains incomplete as long as the ethical dimension and the understanding of liberation are not rooted in a religious tradition.

NOTES

Abridged by the editor. The complete version is to appear in the author's *Theology and Social Theory* (New York: Paulist, 1987).

1. Max Scheler, *Die Wissensformen und die Gesellschaft* (Bern: Francke, 1960); Karl Mannheim, *Ideology and Utopia* (London: Routledge, 1954).
2. Max Weber, *Basic Concepts in Sociology* (New York: Citadel, 1969), p. 29.
3. Alfred Schutz, *The Phenomenology of the Social World* (Evanston, Ill.: Northwestern University Press, 1967).
4. Peter Berger, Hansfried Kellner, *Sociology Reinterpreted* (New York: Doubleday, 1981), especially pp. 17-55.
5. Jacques Ellul, *The Technological Society* (New York: Knopf, 1964).
6. John Badertscher, "George Grant and Jacques Ellul on Freedom in Technological Society," in *George Grant in Process,* ed. Larry Schmidt (Toronto: Anansi, 1978), pp. 79-89, and Douglas Hall, "The Significance of Grant's Cultural Analysis for Christian Theology in North America," in *op. cit.,* pp. 120-129. See also Douglas Hall, *Lighten our Darkness: Towards an Indigenous Theology of the Cross* (Philadelphia: Westminster, 1976).
7. Cf. the work of the development economist, Denis Goulet, for instance his "Obstacles to World Development: An Ethical Reflection," *World Development* 11 (7), pp. 609-624, and "Can Values Shape Third World Technological Policy?" *Journal of International Affairs* 33 (Spring 1979), pp. 50-73. Recently Marxist development economists themselves have discovered the crucial significance of the cultural factor. See Peter Worsley, *The Three Worlds: Culture and World Development* (London: Weidenfeld and Nicolson, 1984).
8. *From Max Weber,* ed. H. H. Gerth and C. W. Mills (New York: Oxford, 1958), pp. 143-144.
9. G. Baum, "Does the World Remain Disenchanted?", *Social Research* 37 (1970), pp. 153-202.
10. G. Baum, *Religion and Alienation* (New York: Paulist, 1975), pp. 58-59.
11. G. Baum, "Science and Commitment: Historical Truth According to Ernst Troeltsch," *Journal of Philosophy of the Social Sciences* 1 (1971), pp. 259-277, reprinted in G. Baum, *The Social Imperative* (New York: Paulist, 1979), pp. 231-254.
12. Max Horkheimer and Theodor Adorno, *Dialectic of Enlightenment* (New York: Herder and Herder, 1969).
13. Paul Tillich, *The Socialist Decision* (New York: Harper and Row, 1977).
14. According to the Canadian Catholic bishops, "As Christians we are called to follow Jesus by identifying with the victims of injustice, by analysing the dominant attitudes and structures that cause human suffering and by actively supporting the poor and oppressed in their struggle to transform society," *Ethical Reflections on the Economic Crisis,* n. 1, in G. Baum and D. Cameron, *Ethics and Economics* (Toronto: Lorimer, 1984), p. 4.

SOCIAL SCIENCE AS MORAL INQUIRY

Yi-Fu Tuan

A unique characteristic of human beings is their moral sense, which affects every aspect of their feeling, thought, and behaviour. From this it follows that if we are to understand society we must consider the moral sense. But what does "moral" mean? I see three sets of meanings. First, moral–as in *mores*, a term popular with anthropologists–signifies accepted practices and customs. In the Western world, moral has also acquired (since the seventeenth century) a preeminently sexual meaning: good morals suggest respectable behaviour in the sexual sphere, and immoral acts immediately call to mind sexual transgressions. But sexual custom is only one custom in the repertoire of a group, albeit a very important one. This special meaning is too confining for the larger aims of social science. To pursue such aims fruitfully, we need to reaffirm the sense of moral as a general, "cover" term for the widely accepted habits and practices of a people. Under this broad definition, anthropologists and cultural geographers have been studying society's morals for a long time; hence, to characterize an important undertaking of social science as moral inquiry, as I have done in the title of this paper, hardly adds anything new. If the characterization nevertheless seems unusual, it is because we have retained in our subconscious the narrow, sexual, and judgmental meaning of the word *moral*.

While most people most of the time take the practices of their culture for granted, some individuals some of the time may question them: they wonder how the practices have originated, what they really mean, and in what ways they are compatible or incompatible with each other. When an individual wonders thus, we say that he or she is engaged in thinking reflectively or philosophically: morality, no longer taken for granted, has become a problem. This is the second sense of moral. A moral being is someone morally awake, alive to the problems of justice, the dilemma of having to choose between competing values, and the need to formulate, however tentatively, some general principles. Nevertheless, it may happen that such an individual will consider these questions only as a sort of intellectual game, with no important consequences on behaviour. Academic philosophers are commonly of this persuasion; and as evidence we may note that their lives are seldom transformed by the issues and conclusions of their own work. Beyond the walls of academe I would assume that people driven to raise moral questions do so not because they provide amusing and challenging puzzles but because the hard facts of day-to-day living make them urgently pressing and real.

Dilemmas appear that almost desperately need to be resolved, but since resolutions, if one were honest and rigorous in thought, are difficult to come by, we may well wonder why people allow themselves this kind of burdensome consciousness at all, and that if it emerges unasked, why they do not quickly suppress it and turn to consoling precedents. The answer is that with rare exceptions, people in fact suppress those glimmers of moral insight that threaten to expand uncomfortably their ethico-intellectual horizons. In any society, the very few who struggle to fan the glimmers are probably able to do so because, in the first place, they are fortunate enough to possess the necessary material and psychological security; and, more importantly, because they possess a love for and a loyalty to a vision of the good. This good is the third meaning of moral. A moral person is a good person, someone capable of transcending the customs when necessary. But to the question of how can one develop the concept of good, form a clearer picture of it, the answer from serious thinkers tends to be disappointing: either it is given in generalities or it elicits an eloquent silence–"it" being the realm "that cannot be said," to quote one authority, Ludwig Wittgenstein.[1]

The good is ineffable: images and words provide, at most, hints of a quality and a direction. Here are a few hints or pointers, directed not at what the good inherently is but at what it can do. As personal experience, the good can appear to us as a distant, luminous goal–approachable yet unattainable–that draws us on. From the standpoint of society, the advantage of holding a powerfully alluring but unspecified idea of the good is that it can encourage society to continue to refine and develop its particular moral precepts, which will therefore not run the danger of being taken as final. For the scholar, the advantage of keeping in mind this third meaning of moral, on top of the other two, is that it enables him to postpone a premature acceptance of moral relativism. Hasty acceptance draws down the curtain of intellectual discourse too soon: it forecloses the exploration of what human beings can potentially achieve. One way to understand social science as moral inquiry is to see it as tentative probes into the moral stature of human individuals and groups–of, in the large view, humanity itself. What are the constraints? What are the possibilities?

Morality and Power

Moral issues are closely tied to power, its use and abuse. Power governs the web of intricate relationships in a group, and is applied externally to nature. Human groups differ greatly in the power at their command. Let us consider a few of them, beginning with those small foraging-hunting bands that possess minimal power. Typically, they are egalitarian and peaceful. Members of such a band have to cooperate to survive; and this cooperation cannot be given grudgingly if a certain genial atmosphere, desirable in itself but perhaps also necessary to survival, is to be sustained. So, signs of affection are overt and frequently expressed. Much touching and fondling occur not only between adults and children but also between adults. However, tensions and conflicts of a mild kind do exist even in these Eden-like worlds. One potential cause of disharmony is that power and prestige tend to accrue naturally to individuals who are superior in strength, skill or knowledge. In an egalitarian band, this tendency must be nipped in the bud by techniques of belittling, which are of course a form of aggression. Another source of tension is living in close physical proximity. Togetherness is considered highly desirable; nonetheless people can and do get into each other's hair. Irritation is manifest in teasing, a certain violence in the use of language, and practical jokes. Such occurrences are at odds with the socially recognized ideals of harmony, of gentleness in expression and behaviour, and of silence or song. Thus even in the simplest hunting band, ideal and reality can be in conflict. Mildly aggressive acts do not, however, threaten the integrity of the group: in fact, they contribute toward group integrity by providing a harmless outlet for unavoidable frustrations. The people themselves seem unaware of moral paradoxes. Awarding a brave hunter's success with a sneer is not something to be puzzled over and resolved.[2]

Although the human band necessarily feeds on nature, disturbance of the natural setting is minimal. Only a trained eye can detect the slight modifications in vegetation and fauna that might have occurred. Among the foraging-hunting bands of the tropical rain forests, the Tasaday of Mindanao Island in the Philippines had the least power over nature. They were foragers rather than hunters. The largest animals they habitually killed for food were frogs. Their one recognized enemy in the animal world was the snake. When they encountered a snake in the forest they preferred to run away rather than try to kill it. The peaceableness of the Tasaday thus seems to have extended to the animals themselves. They truly appear to be a people out of Eden. The simplicity of their world was not only material but also mythological, religious, and ceremonial. If the Tasaday minimized killing, it was not because their religion forbade it. It was because they lacked the tools.

When trapping techniques and tools for hunting were introduced, the Tasaday quickly became efficient at capturing large animals such as the deer, which they once regarded as their friend: the killing and disembowelment of a friend did not arouse excessive feelings of guilt.[3]

A simple and idyllic life, egalitarian and full of warmth and caring toward all members young and old, characterized another hunting band, the Semang of Malaya. The Semang were technically more advanced than the Tasaday. They had, for instance, the death-dealing blowpipe. Their ethical values also seem more developed. They had formulated an attitude toward animals that was gentle and solicitous. It was considered a great offense, punishable by serious illness, to mistreat captured animals or even to laugh at them. Game brought down with a blowpipe had to be killed quickly and without pain.[4] As in most hunting bands in tropical and subtropical latitudes, the main source of food for the Semang was plants collected by the women rather than game killed by the men. The plant world rather than the fauna supported the bulk of the needs for human life. Given this fact, it should be easy for a people such as the Semang to avoid formulating an ethics toward animals at all. Animals could simply be killed when the desire for meat arose and then be forgotten. There was no compelling reason why putting animals to death should burden the conscience of the Semang, but it did, and this fact is a credit to the sensitivity of their moral imagination.

Eskimos, unlike the hunting bands of lower latitudes, were completely dependent on animals for almost every aspect of their needs–food, clothing, and shelter. Eskimos were superbly skilled hunters. Excellence in any field of endeavour presupposes enjoyment. Eskimos no doubt enjoyed chasing down game, thrusting their spear and knife into a warm body, disemboweling it. Yet these acts of violence were not totally acceptable to the culture: they *had* to be accepted as part of the harshness of life in the Arctic. A popular legend concerning the origin of sea mammals hints at the malaise. "Villagers piled on to a raft to move to another hunting area as the one they lived in was exhausted of game. This was a most trying time for all. As the raft moved to the open waters it began to sink because it carried too many people. To lighten the load, an orphaned girl was thrown overboard. She clung to the edge of the raft, hoping to be allowed to climb back. Someone picked up a knife and lopped off her fingers. She slipped into the depth of the sea where her fingers turned into sea mammals. The little girl herself became the Spirit of the Sea and patron of its animals. Her sympathy to the needs of human beings, predictably, was limited."[5] Hunters who, after a strenuous outing, failed to make a kill, or who were drowned at sea could hardly complain. The story thus serves to make the cruelty of Arctic life predictable and in a sense just–the pitiless justice of necessity. Nonetheless, a feeling of guilt remains. Animals, unprovoked, rarely harm human beings. The injury is one-sided. Human beings kill. Is the lack of choice a sufficient excuse? Morality in the second sense, we have noted earlier, is this awareness of a dilemma which may lead to attempts at formulating general moral principles.

In general, Eskimo culture discourages thinking about moral dilemmas. To what purpose? they would say. Who can solve them? Great and difficult questions are better avoided. Just as the earth grows angry when men take too many stones and too much turf in the making of their meat stores, so the spirits that control human fate may be offended if men concern themselves with deep questions. Apart from eating, resting, and sleeping, human beings know very little; and it might easily seem presumptuous if they endeavour to form opinions about hidden things. Happy folk should not worry themselves by thinking.[6] These words of wisdom from the world of the Iglulik Eskimos possibly hold good for all cultures, including our own. The examined life, most people agree through their words and action, is not worth living. Only a small minority in any culture, driven by talent or temperament and secure in livelihood, move beyond the consolations of custom to confront the imponderables of life, among which one of the most acute and persistent is the killing of animals.

Building Worlds

As we have seen, Eskimos hold the belief that the earth might grow angry if men take too many stones from it to build shelters and meat stores. This is simply one example out of many which shows how a people can experience doubt and guilt in exercising power over nature. Scholars have not sufficiently taken this ambivalence into account. We are perhaps too absorbed by the idea, argued so strongly by Claude Lévi-Strauss, that people everywhere recognize a distinction between nature and culture, and that it is culture that is esteemed: esteemed is the "cooked" rather than the "raw," the uniquely human, the cosmeticized, rather than the undefined and the wild. But when we examine those aspects of culture which garner indisputable prestige, we find that they tend to be the "intangibles," such things as language, lineage, rules of behaviour, ceremony and ritual, songs and legends, rather than the material constructs of culture: paths, fields, huts, and temples.[7] A large building such as the men's house, a shrine or a temple, certainly carries prestige, but the source of that prestige does not lie in the physical structure so much as in what the structure accommodates–men of power, ancestral spirits, and nature deities. Insofar as the building itself emanates a certain numinous aura, it does so at the time of construction, for in many societies the act of construction is itself a sacred event; and it does so again when a ritual is performed within the building's compass. At other times, the shrine or temple may be treated quite differently as just another shelter.[8] We know that an agricultural people, even if their tools and methods of cultivation are primitive, can over time significantly change nature: we know that their clearings and abandoned clearings can leave a more or less enduring mark on the face of the earth. But, although such simple cultivators may be proud of their customs and traditions, they almost invariably overlook their culture's largest work–the transformed landscape, which they tend to regard as an unvarying, almost natural, feature of their environment.

Civilization is power over nature. It imposes a secondary world on the primary one. If we look at civilized people's physical actions alone, in China as in Europe, this power would appear to have been exercised without hesitation and at times with brutal insensitivity: vast expanses of forest are felled, rocks and minerals dug out of the mountains, rivers diverted and channeled. This is a familiar theme. But if we look at what is thought and said–at the literature of a civilization–we find moralists in all periods of history severely criticizing the aspirations of high culture. At the deepest and oldest level of sentience, there lurked the common fear of impiety: digging into the earth and putting proud, highrising structures on top of it–unless they were dedicated to the gods themselves–were clearly impious acts. Human sacrifice eased the anxiety. Strange as it may now seem to us, this ancient practice continued in Europe, here and there and increasingly surreptitiously, until modern times–until, that is, the last alleged occurrence in 1871, when Lord Leigh was accused of having built a person into the foundations of a bridge at Stoneleigh in Warwickshire.[9]

Dread of committing impiety constituted the deepest layer of ambivalence. Later, a more explicit, reasoned, and humane expression of doubt emerged. In China as well as in Europe, moralists took to denouncing the grander aspects of high civilization–the palaces and great gardens, the royal retreats and capitals–not because they offended the gods but because they signified human vainglory: moreover, the critics saw that these edifices could only be built by exploiting the people and the land, inflicting death and extreme hardship on the one, while exhausting the resources of the other. Traditional thought did not allow for the possibility that a dedicated, rational, and systematic effort to transform nature could benefit everyone, rich and poor, in the long run. It was taken for granted that whatever the potentates used was used up at the expense of the people and the living earth. The entire secondary world of human creation commanded only a limited respect from the philosophers. To them, a landscape of cultivated fields and houses spoke primarily of the necessity of livelihood: this particular aspect of the secondary world had no great value in itself, and warranted esteem only to the extent that it gave indispensable support to a measured life of civility and social harmony. As for the grand architecture in the secondary world, we have already noted that it signified luxury and vainglory, built and maintained irrespective of cost to people and nature.

In traditional belief and thought, the human will is deeply suspect. It suggests willfulness–a determination to impose and change the course of things. Will is passion; whenever it is allowed its sway it leads almost inevitably to deviation and excess. In China, thinkers as different as Confucius, Mo-tzu, and the propounders of Taoism subscribed, in varying degree, to a philosophy of minimal deliberative action (wu wei). Buildings must not be too large and government at all levels should be light and barely felt. When good social order prevails it operates like nature, without force or strain, spontaneously. Even speech that issues commands and rules may not be necessary; and if it turns out to be necessary, then that in itself is evidence of failure. Confucius, so concerned with being effective–with reforming the governments of his time–nevertheless said: "I would prefer not to speak. Does Heaven speak? The four seasons pursue their course; all things are produced by it, but does Heaven speak?"[10]

If nonliterate peoples are proud of their lineage and customs rather than of the secondary worlds they have created, what are the things considered good by thinkers in highly developed, traditional societies? Again, lineage and custom. In China, for instance, Confucians are proud of the li, that is, of those humane and aesthetically-pleasing rules that govern all levels of social behaviour, from day-to-day etiquette to high ritual. But, in addition, thoughtful people in high cultures take pride in philosophical discourse, in a contemplative appreciation of nature, and in art. Significantly, none of these activities requires any large-scale material transformations of the primary world. Force need not be used. Will is held in abeyance. Beauty and the good are not in conflict. Indeed, for Plato, most people can be led to the good only through the lure of beauty, by which he means the stars and the perfectly shaped bodies of young humans; and, of course, these are not the sort of things that can be manufactured by mortals. The question of power–of destroying matter so as to recreate it into a more desirable form–does not arise. Plato goes to the extreme of disapproving, for moral reasons, the arts, including poetry and painting. Most moralists are less severe: to them, the arts at their best are glimmers into truth, and even if this be disallowed they are a playful and harmless pastime.[11]

Albrecht Dürer wrote: "Observe nature industriously, conform to it, and do not deviate from it thinking that you know how to find it better by yourself, for then you are misled...."[12] This was the traditional, humble attitude of the human artisan and artist. True creation is God's prerogative alone: man's work is to conform with God's creation–nature.

Yet, by and large, the Renaissance was a time when as the force of religion receded Europeans began to be boastful of their own creations at all scales up to the secular splendors of the city, including the palaces and gardens, the libraries and stables, the plazas and avenues. Excess no longer seemed a fault. Pride draped over the secondary world, first primarily over the cities, later (from the eighteenth century onward) over the prosperous countryside as well. This pride in the secondary world of human manufacture reached an apogee in the nineteenth century. But it did not last. Indeed, deep doubts were expressed even in the nineteenth century. Why are certain buildings considered good or beautiful, and others not? What is the relationship between beauty and the good? Is the good the "organic" ? If so, Gothic architecture is inherently good, and a contorted argument might be used to back up this belief. Is the good an expression of a freedom of choice? Then an eclectic style is the good. Is it a sort of authenticity and honesty that disdains the sterile social symbolism of a hierarchical past? Then a plain, functional style using contemporary technology is the good.[13] The countryside cannot totally escape this new consciousness and controversy. An issue that emerged in the nineteenth century and which remains very much alive today is the relative merit of "organic" versus "chemical" farming. At stake here are not only questions of efficiency and productivity but also an inchoate sense of nonarbitrary virtue that human beings seem unable to live without.

Morality of Exchange

Human relations are at the heart of morality. I should like to turn now to the morality of exchange–the kinds of exchange that hold human groups together and that lie at the basis of their power, including power over nature that I have already sketched. Exchanges occur by means of body gesture: thus, we touch each other, fondle, smile, raise a hand, pluck at our ear lobe, and so on. Often this particular form of exchange takes place below the level of consciousness: unknown to ourselves, we may be cementing or terminating a relationship from the way we stand, or tilt the chin. Exchanges occur, of course, by means of words; and words, from their multi-layered meanings and from the way they are said, are soaked through with emotion-tinted values, with praise, imprecations, and judgments. In ordinary social conversation, almost nothing that we say is neutral–a mere capsule of information; almost everything we say–again often unknown to ourselves–subtly adds to or detracts from, by however minute a degree, a relationship. Because everything we do with stance, gesture, or word carries moral signals and may have moral effects, human reality is at every point moral. We act as moral beings whether we are fully aware of doing so or not. Most of our behaviour is probably undeliberated and subconscious; much of it, however, *is* deliberate: we deliberately smile, shake hands, or say something pleasing in order to be rewarded with similar gestures and thus establish a bond. Now, by contrast with the exchange of gestures and words, the exchange of material things is almost always a conscious process. Sometimes this consciousness emerges as self-centered calculation. In a traditional village community, the character of a gift exchange tends to be well-defined: six chickens for a lamb, three hogs for a calf. In a more complex hierarchical society, calculation may be even more deliberative and elaborate, for the nature and value of the gift has to be carefully calibrated with the status of the recipient. The recipient may be one's protector, patron or landlord, or he may be a local deity–a spirit of nature that can bestow benefit–in which case the gift is called an offering. The point here is that, for all the pious words and gestures of a sacrificial rite, the exchange remains at the practical level of material benefit. Cato's advice in *De agricultura*, for example, makes this clear: the presentation of an offering is like the application of a fertilizer–a practical technique to guarantee success in farming.

Yet, even when the aim of a gift exchange is self-centered and worldly, it is still capable of generating human warmth and bond, a sense of duty and of obligation. It would seem that people cannot share, for whatever motive, without creating a feeling of mutuality and perhaps even a tolerant affection for each other. Furthermore, numerous exceptions to the practice of strict accounting no doubt exist. One might like to explore those cases in which the idea of "increase" holds: for instance, a little more sugar is returned than was borrowed, and borrowed tools are given back shining, that is, in even better condition than before. However, the irony is that such acts of generosity are inevitably tied to calculation: in the very process of the exchange, neighbours have to keep in mind that one cup of sugar was received and hence one-and-a-half cup must be returned. How can people escape such seemingly unworthy accounting? It is reassuring to know that at least two kinds of gift exist which bring forth increase and which, in addition, have the merit of defying precise calculation. One is the gift of live animals and the other is the gift of ideas or knowledge. Both "goods" increase naturally, or have the potential of doing so. Both, traditionally, have been considered of exceptional value. Potentates, for instance, have always offered each other rare animals as tokens of mutual esteem, and nations still do so: thus the American musk ox is exchanged for the Chinese panda. As for the gift of life-enhancing knowledge, that benefaction has established, in times past, the high standing of the teacher vis-à-vis his pupil; and in our own time the imparting of technical knowledge from one country to another is regarded as invaluable assistance–a true gesture of friendship.

Exchange may be between two persons. This can deteriorate into a calculating and sterile sort of *égoisme à deux* (D. H. Lawrence's phrase): no real largesse of spirit, kindness, generosity or surprise is involved. Binary reciprocity can, of course, also be a model of care and piety. The best known example is the parent-child relationship in which the flow of care in one direction is reversed in the course of time, out of love and gratitude. What makes this reciprocity generous is the lack of an accounting based on narrow self-interest. But, despite such well-known exceptions, reciprocation of goods and services between only two individuals tends to become quickly mechanical and degenerate into mutual back-scratching. Much more liberating and productive is circular giving (Lewis Hyde's term), which involves a number of individuals, some and perhaps most of whom are strangers.[14] Under such condition, an individual has to give blindly, with no assurance that benefit will eventually flow back to oneself, and certainly with no assurance as to the time when a particular act of giving will return to one as reward. In general, the larger and more complex a society, the larger the circles of exchange. In a modern society, the circle may grow so extended that to the giver it appears linear: a gesture is thrown to the winds and one never quite knows what will transpire. Where the exchange is strictly for profit, as in a commercial enterprise, the businessman's venture capital constitutes his willingness to take risk: notwithstanding all the information and technical analysis he receives he has no guarantee that his investment will bring him profit. This willingness to take risk in business life–and, for that matter, in any venture in which the outcome is unsure–provides a curious analogue for impulses in the moral realm: I refer to that spirit of giving and assistance which does not and cannot expect any immediate return, or even foresee, clearly, the outcome. The analogue offered here is embarrassing because we do not care to juxtapose the materialist and the moral realms, and yet only dreamers can believe that they do not mirror, and have tangible links with, each other.

Epilogue

Social reality can be modeled in a variety of ways. One way, currently popular, is to see it as games and performances. The games may be consciously played for social and economic advantages, and for the sheer fun of power–the power to initiate and manipulate; and they may also be played subconsciously, that is, without any awareness that certain goals are being pursued. A scholar's task is to describe and interpret these games. A peculiar sophistication of our time is that the scholar no longer claims, as he used to do, that his account and interpretation represent knowledge: he is hesitant to assert that his text, for all the unavoidable distortions and inaccuracies, is in essentials a correct picture of reality, one that the actors themselves are almost certainly not fully aware of. In the present intellectual climate, the scholar's text tends to be viewed as though it were a work of art–a construction using whatever facts are available–that can be commended for its inherent qualities of coherence and insight quite apart from whether it conforms to the real. This conception is unambiguously put by the anthropologist Edmund Leach: "Anthropological texts are interesting in themselves and not because they tell us something about the external world."[15]

"Interesting." This word, by now, is one of the weakest in the English lexicon. Do we scholars and social scientists labour for no greater aim than to produce something "interesting" ? Actually, I do not doubt for a moment that researchers continue to believe that they contribute to knowledge. What seems deeply problematical to contemporary students of the human scene is the feeling that the knowledge they produce lacks import and application; and a reason for this feeling is the still barely formulated belief that the fundamental *fact* concerning human reality is already known. It is already known that people play games, about which we can only say that some are more elaborate or ingenious than others; some are played with vigour, others languidly; some last longer than others. Ethically speaking these different scenarios and games are stretched out along a horizontal plane; we are enervated by the conviction that any attempt at vertical arrangement is out of order. Now, I endorse the theatrical or "game" model of human reality. Though not the only possible model, it has the merit of testability in ordinary experience and also perhaps the merit of fruitfulness. I suggest, however, one important modification, namely, that when we study people in the real world we look upon what they do, not as we would any play but as we would a morality play. A morality play may contain amusement and even farce, but it is fundamentally serious. It is supposed to offer a lesson, which for modern men and women cannot be a set of precepts or a religio-ethical system however subtly and elevatingly formulated: it can only be a reminder for us to keep alive an attitude of tolerance and receptivity toward an open-ended concept of the good.

NOTES

1. Paul Engelmann, *Letters from Ludwig Wittgenstein* (Oxford: Blackwell, 1967), pp. 97-98.
2. Richard Lee, "Eating Christmas in the Kalahari," *Natural History* (December 1969); Eleanor Leacock and Richard Lee, eds., *Politics and History in Band Societies* (Cambridge: Cambridge University Press, 1982).
3. John Nance, *The Gentle Tasaday* (New York: Harcourt, Brace, Jovanovich, 1975), p. 274.

4. Iskander Carey, *Orang Asli: The Aboriginal Tribes of Peninsular Malaysia* (Kuala Lumpur, Singapore: Oxford University Press, 1976), p. 99.

5. Asen Balikci, *The Netsilik Eskimo* (Garden City, New York: Natural History Press, 1970), p. 206.

6. Knud Rasmussen, *Intellectual Culture of the Iglulik Eskimos, Report of the Fifth Thule Expedition, 1921-24*, 7 (No. 1, 1929), p. 69.

7. Carol P. MacCormack, "Nature, Culture and Gender: A Critique," in Carol P. MacCormack and Marilyn Strathern, eds., *Nature, Culture and Gender* (Cambridge: Cambridge University Press, 1980), p. 16.

8. As one example, see J. M. Schoffeleers, "Cult Idioms and the Dialectics of a Region," in R. P. Werbner, ed., *Regional Cults* (London: Academic Press, 1977), p. 219.

9. Lord Raglan, *The Temple and the House* (New York: Norton, 1964), p. 19.

10. Arthur Waley, *The Analects of Confucius* (New York: Random House, Vintage Books, 1938), book 17, chapter 19, p. 214. See Benjamin Schwartz, *The World of Thought in Ancient China* (Cambridge: Harvard University Press, 1985).

11. Iris Murdoch, *The Fire and the Sun: Why Plato Banished the Artists* (Oxford: Clarendon, 1977).

12. Johan Huizinga, *Men and Ideas: History, the Middle Ages, the Renaissance* (Princeton: Princeton University Press, 1984), p. 302.

13. David Watkin, *Morality and Architecture* (Oxford: Clarendon, 1977).

14. Lewis Hyde, *The Gift: Imagination and the Erotic Life of Property* (New York: Random House, Vintage Books, 1983).

15. Edmund Leach, "Glimpses of the Unmentionable in the History of British Social Anthropology," *Annual Review of Anthropology* 13 (1984), p. 22.

6

TOWARD A HUMANIST HISTORY
OF SEX

Serge Gagnon

For twenty years I have been accumulating expressions of the subjectivity of my fellow historians. Both personally and in book reviews, colleagues have not ceased to pass along their annoyance with my essays in historiography. Their questions boil down to this: what are you driving at? I feel obliged to respond at last.

In the foreword and the two final chapters of my *Quebec and Its Historians, the Twentieth Century,*[1] I believe I have set forth the conditions under which one can practice an historical science free, in so far as possible, of our prejudices, value judgments, and other "projections of ourselves." But in taking this step in my intellectual journey,[2] in asserting my own prejudice for the New History, a history more scientific and less present-oriented, I have not veered from my humanist concerns. The *how* of the science of history can never eliminate the crucial question of *why*. In this respect I ally myself with that epistemology of relevance so often affirmed by Fernand Dumont.[3] Can one do humanist history? If so, by what procedures, what inquiries, what approach, or as we say in French, what *problematique*? I accepted the invitation to contribute here because I am in the midst of two studies which I expect can be described as humanist. Both are set at the beginning of the nineteenth century. The one (*Death, Priest, Suicide*) is intended as a history of the meaning of suffering in premodern societies, and of the value placed on it. The other seeks to reformulate the dialectic between licit and illicit with respect to customs of sexual pleasure prior to the era of dechristianization.[4] I will refer to the latter inquiry in disclosing the philosophy that guides me.

Sexuality and Religious Faith According to the Prevailing Epistemology

For the dechristianized West, the historical relation between sexuality and religious faith is difficult to define outside a framework that pits the repression of the past against the freedom of today. Yet some rare historians think it likely that sexual ascetism, not always realized of course but held up as an ideal, was the keystone of the rise of the West. The learning of sexual discipline, from constraint of auto-eroticism in adolescence to the periodic abstinence imposed by monogamy, was a rule of conduct inspired by both Bible and tradition. This was the sexual culture the priest proposed and the great mass of the faithful received. The success of this colossal effort of acculturation occurred in successive waves. Splendidly recapitulated by Georges Duby,[5] the obsession with millenarian purity was the outcome of the first stage in the history of customs governing sexual pleasure. The second great step forward came from the Reformation.

This scenario, which would show the positive effect of moral theology (while recognizing its excesses), has few adherents, so far as I know, among Western specialists in the social sciences. Authors of the time spoke of ethical requirements, but we see only constraints on free enjoyment. In the history of the relation between sexuality and religious faith, top billing goes to the notion that a theological sexology is repressive. Further, the psychologism of our twentieth century does its part toward constructing an epistemology that takes the death of God as paradigmatic. Here, as in much else, philosophy has led the way. Nietzsche, among others, made a virulent indictment of Christianity.[6] Like Marx, Nietzsche thought belief had been used for purposes of domination by the ruling class. But unlike the logician of the British Museum, who simply identified faith as foolishness, Nietzsche went further, designating the realm of emotions as the religious domain. Wanting to free the human psyche of morality, he identified faith and neurosis before psychoanalytic discourse had yet established itself: "Everywhere that religious neurosis appears..., we find it linked to three dangerous states: solitude, youth, and continence." He likened the "Christian infection" to a "latent form of epilepsy," and parodied the voluntary self-denial of the ascetic, who pretends to act with the Kingdom of God in mind, but who is in fact "the fanatic enemy of nature."[7]

The Nietzschean way of disposing with Christian morality paved the way for analytic psychology. Nietzsche influenced Freud,[8] notably with regard to pleasure disguised as pain in Christian discourse on sexuality. Freudian analysis faced the question of the normality of sexual abstinence, whether in adolescence, as a permanent option in adult life, or as periodic continence. Is sublimation possible without upsetting the workings of body and mind? Freud hesitated in his answer. At one moment he took as given that one cannot resist the TRIEB, the "irresistible pressure" in which the sex drive consists. Then in another passage he maintained that sublimation is possible without danger to mental health: the individual can manage this by redirecting or converting the sex drive into creative energy invested in work, politics, religiosity, art, or whatever.

Historical demographers like Pierre Chaunu and André Burguière have subscribed to such a view.[9] In the opposite camp, Jacques Solé and Jean-Louis Flandrin have in varying degrees adopted the idea that one cannot resist the sex drive without suffering more or less painful psychosomatic maladies.[10] The debate took place about a statistic confirming a drop in illegitimate births during the Old Regime even in the midst of a rise in the age of marriage. For Flandrin, the lessening of fruitful heterosexual relations attested by the decline in pregnancies and births before or outside marriage did not imply a lessening of sexual activity among French peasants. Birth-control practices spilled over into rural France before the Revolution. This first wave of sexual freedom was expressed in an alleged increase in "masturbatory" practices. Answering critics of this thesis, Flandrin called as witness the founder of psychoanalysis:

> I do not see by what reading of Freud one can pull out such a theory of sublimation. On the contrary, I read in one of his articles of 1908: "Our hoary culture requires of the lonely man and woman abstinence until marriage, and lifelong abstinence unless they contract legitimate marriage. What the authorities want to affirm, that such abstinence is neither harmful nor very difficult, many physicians have also held.... But only a minority achieves *self-mastery through sublimation*, by the diversion of the sex drive toward higher cultural ends–and then only sporadically, and with all the greater difficulty in the period of juvenile hot-bloodedness. Most of the others become neurotic or suffer various harms. Experience shows that most people were not cut out for the duty of abstinence."[11]

Flandrin's works generally corroborate the viewpoint just quoted. This historian of sexuality maintains, for example, that the priests of the Old Regime believed married men incapable of doing without sexual relations for more than a few days.[12] In his analysis of the alleged sexuality of unmarried eighteenth-century youth in the French countryside, Flandrin holds that for the most part, they engaged in regular sexual activity including solitary masturbation, withdrawal during intercourse, and other practices not resulting in childbirth.[13]

It seems curious that Flandrin relied on Freud to refute the position of Burguière and Chaunu. Wilhelm Reich's thought seems to me much more in line with Flandrin's estimation of the harmfulness, or indeed impossibility, of sublimation. Raising historical materialism to the level of cultural analysis, Reich's oft-reprinted *The Sexual Revolution* prophesied during the 1930s what Edward Shorter has called the second Western sexual revolution–the one we are now living, since the advent of chemical contraceptives and the spread of their use from adolescence on. For

Chaunu, contraception, abortion, and sterilization set the stage for a structural change without precedent in the history of our civilization: the separation of sexual pleasure from procreation.[14]

Whatever Flandrin may think, Freud did in fact uphold the idea that sexuality can be sublimated, diverted from hedonistic ends, converted into creative energy, and invested in artistic, political, humanitarian, or other causes. In Reich's view, Freud's philosophy of culture, in much the same was as "Stoic-Christian sexual ethics" (Flandrin's phrase), blocks individual development and even threatens the public peace:

> Repressing sexuality amounts to upsetting the fundamental vital functions not only in a medical sense, but in a more general way. Its most important social expression is irrationality in human action: mysticism, religiosity, inclination to war, and so on.[15]

In sum, the effects of sexual repression would be religious "foolishness," violence, and militarism. In this regard, Reich gave an account of his clinical observations. His patients arrived bridled by guilt, the "coercive ethic" of the duty of premarital and extramarital abstinence. This religiously inspired "ascetic morality" with its "fear of hell-fire" made healthy constitutions sink into neurosis. Reich considered the vast majority of human beings neurotic, their mental illness engendered by abstinence in adolescence, monogamy, and "required marriage" (required, that is, to gain access to sexual pleasure). Reich, moreover, indicted Freudian psychoanalysis for placing sexuality and culture in opposition, for regarding the repression of instinct as the well-spring of culture, and for attributing cultural achievements to the sublimation of sexual energy.[16] In opposition to Freud, Reich considered that the frequency and intensity of orgasms increase human productivity many times over, and that to believe in the creative potential of repressed sexual energy is wrong.

Might not Reich have understood Freud better than Flandrin? Might not Flandrin be identifying himself perhaps unknowingly with Reichian positions whose influence is lodged in the pansexuality of our day, in therapy, and in the dominant epistemology–as, for example, in Margaret Mead's oft-reprinted account of adolescence in Samoa? Reich pled for sexual activity without constraint, whenever the human being is gripped by arousal of the sex drive. In this perspective, to forgo the release of orgasm would be hazardous to psychosomatic equilibrium. That is why Freudian therapy is suspect–it acts as guardian of the old, Stoic-Christian morality described as "compulsive" or "obsessive." Reich proposed "regulation according to sexual economy." Pedophilia, homosexuality, and bestiality are rare forms of sexual pleasure judged abnormal, and Reich considers them perverse effects of a repressive society. With these exceptions, he recommends "the rejection of every rule."[17]

The spread of "Reichism" has led to extreme positions in the liberalization of the market of sexual change. For many today, it is hard to imagine two people being close without desire for a sexual transaction. Philippe Ariès argued that the pansexuality of this late twentieth century is embraced to the detriment of the sentiment of friendship. Friendship, Ariès wrote, "has even been loaded with conscious sexuality, making it naive, ambiguous, or shameful. Society condemns it between men too dissimilar in age: today, Hemingway's old man and child, returning from their journey at sea, would arouse the suspicions of the vice squad and of mothers."[18] That a professional Canadian psychologist should become a promoter of "beneficial" pedophilia and that a journalist should be condemned by the Quebec Press Council for having "insulted" the psychologist on camera, indicate the extent of our "tolerance" in sexual matters. Rare are those who recognize in the sex drive a power that can even destroy oneself or other people if culture does not harness and educate it for a developing sexual encounter–a prospect in jeopardy without self-control. Such a moral philosophy need not be specifically Christian. Even pre-Christian societies in Greece and Rome had developed such a view, as Michel Foucault pointed out in his last essays.[19]

The sexual mentality that so disturbed Ariès is precisely what one finds in a great many scholarly works. It is the interpretive leaven in Jacques Solé's book on love in the modern Western world.[20] In this same spirit Jean-Paul Aron has written a history of masturbation.[21] One could cite many other examples from the field of history alone. Compared to all these books spread far and wide in the wake of sexual "freedom," essays that recognize the value of voluntary abstinence for the sake of the Kingdom are rare. Odile Arnold's *Le corps et l'âme* seems to be an exception.[22] The mortification of monks and nuns is not there ridiculed or labeled as masochist, but understood as a positive value. But this is a marginal study. The fashion among historians is to account for the choice of lifelong abstinence by "profane" factors. The etiological scenarios vary: fear of childbirth; fear of the penis, in the case of young postulants in the convent who have perhaps experienced incest, pedophilia, or some other traumatising sexual violence; physical ugliness; grinding poverty from which the young woman could not escape if she remained "in the world." Would not factors like these explain her supposedly voluntary withdrawal into religious life? But what if these choices had been freely agreed to by men and women who believe that God exists and that he calls them to their renunciation? To entertain the latter explanation one must, I think, not only postulate the existence of a God who holds out, in the Catholic system, a particularly exacting ideal, but one must also defy academic censure. Understanding requires at the start even a paradigm of misdeed, of sin–without which it seems to me difficult to account for religious experience.[23] Works of this kind are now beginning to appear, works that acknowledge sin as understood in the Catholic system and, until recently, in Western culture at large. These reflect something more than what Michel Foucault and Jacques Donzelot have described as a wish to know that hides a wish for power.[24]

Toward a "Humanist" History of Sex and the Sacred

The project I undertook at the start of this decade will piece together anew the relation between sexuality and religious faith in Quebec, from the early nineteenth century on. The crucial epistemological question haunting me can be formulated thus: how to make good use of an impressive mass of documentation without projecting onto an era long past the sexual values inherent in our own fun morality. How to speak of the Ancients without denouncing the prohibitions formulated by their priests or by other agents of what Marcuse called libidinal rationality. Should one give a prominent place to transgressions in order to show that the peasants paid scant heed to prohibitions? This view of things dominates the historical scholarship of the last ten or twenty years. I have cited Jacques Solé and Jean-Louis Flandrin in the case of France. Lawrence Stone, Edward Shorter, and a whole retinue of scholars are more or less in league with contemporary hedonists in reconstructing the customs of the past. This same moral philosophy runs as a thread through Robert-Lionel Séguin's *La vie libertine en Nouvelle-France.*[25] The rare discordant voices–some thundering, even preaching like Chaunu's– try in opposition to show the positive value of mastery of the sex drive in that earlier time when transgression aroused guilt. The fun morality of the post-war period has made fashionable the opposition between freedom and repression, while consigning to oblivion the correspondence between freedom and responsibility that was a fact in premodern generations. It is indeed hard to understand past populations if one projects onto them the hedonistic values raised to the rank of virtues by the sexual revolution of the past quarter-century.

To the sin of anachronism and the sin of method can be added another that the historian of sexuality risks still more: failure to recognize in the Christianity of the past the dialectic play of the religious and the sexual. Such an attitude amounts to renouncing understanding of the customs of another time. Religiosity gave *meaning* to sexual enjoyment. If you accept that by nature, sexuality is a propulsion toward encounter with another, it is also, in certain respects, a yearning for the Other–or at least it was in traditional societies. During intercourse, the uniting of beings is not truly realized except in the form of a third human life. One should not then wonder at the puzzle surrounding sexual encounter in premalthusian societies, where Eros battled death for the sake of life. Not so long ago, involuntary sterility was a curse, an ignominious infirmity. Without engaging in nostalgia, the historian might at least take into account the negative fallout of the new sexual morality. The techiques of more intense pleasure, reaching now an unprecedented scale in the West, are not grounds to foresee the coming of infinite orgasm–the representation of paradisaic bliss in the Arab-Islamic ethical tradition.

To understand the sexuality of the past, to reconstruct it for Westerners of our time, helping them discover the *meaning* of traditional eroticism, is a very different thing than *denouncing* the castrating work of priests for the sake of glorifying our sexual revolution. It is perhaps to initiate a new dialogue with generations that are gone, and to look for a light, an education where the dominant epistemology sees only darkness and repression, ignorance and denial of pleasure. To set beacons on the historical march, is this not a way of practicing that humanist science of history in which the dead are questioned to learn the secret of their serenity, even their joy? To recount the limits of enjoyment set by culture, limits promoted by the Church–is this not a way to discover that a great part of suffering was positively experienced as a fact of human life? For suffering is not only the product of social conditions, that is, of the relations of subordination produced by people; it is an integral part of human experience. Thus did belief give meaning to suffering equally as to delight.

In company with other specialized, synchronic sciences, history has lost its mission as a purveyor of ethics. Too rare still are those historians of culture who risk proposing to their contemporaries behaviours now passé that once had therapeutic value or a certain morality. Certain recent and great historical essays deserve to be recognized as pioneering works. Ariès conceived of his history of death as a means of giving back to suffering its rightful place in this world. A Canadian physician in charge of palliative care at Royal Victoria Hospital, hence opposed to unremitting therapeutic effort, has paid homage to the French historian and urged the scholarly community to pursue his work:

> We must rehabilitate death, reinvent it, rediscover with the help of historians and poets that richness lost that was...the meaning of death–which was, I suppose, just the meaning of life that we have also lost.... The historians of the world should devote themselves to restoring to us how our ancestors died.... We would no longer have to battle the despicable conspiracy of silence; we would be forced perhaps to care better not for cancer, but for the patient suffering from cancer.[26]

In *The Culture of Narcissism*, Christopher Lasch proposes to his contemporaries directions for living that would cure them of ennui, emptiness, chaos, of the absurdity of Western culture in this twilight of the century. In denouncing the therapeutic society, he has indeed offered a therapy by history. If I read him correctly, he suggests that in middle age it is more worthwhile to keep the good memories of youth, to obtain peacefulness by meditation, music, maybe religion. Is this philosophy of life not more in harmony with the human condition than is a desperate quest for illusory maps to the modern Fountain of Youth? Lasch's book competes with Gail Sheehy's therapeutic best-seller, for he has attempted a psychoanalytic history. He takes up again a venerable tradition, not yet so remote from us, when history claimed to be the mistress of life. It is a new dialogue with the past that a humanist science of history should promote. In any case, this is what I attempt in my endeavour on the history of human sexuality.[27]

Numerous treatises in sexology make the benefit of pleasure the sole measure of sexual habits. In his *Sex and the Single Man*, Albert Ellis expressed, at the start of our sexual revolution, the ethical fundamentals of the fun morality:

> You are not here primarily to achieve something wonderful during your life-time, to be of great service to others, to change the course of the world, or to do anything else but...enjoy yourself.[28]

Successful books like Alex Comfort's *The Joy of Sex* rushed to popularize these new canons. A fundamental ethical change, the sexual revolution has nonetheless disturbed many moralists and certain critical anthropolgists and sociologists.

Sociologist André Béjin, for example, suggests that the new *command* of the "ratebusters of hedonism" is the "duty of orgasm," this imperative arousing guilt, inhibition, and fear of poor performance. Worried, tense, unsatisfied at not being able to multiply or prolong pleasure, the "handicapped" person is delivered to sex therapists vested with the power of repairing dysfunctions. In this context the sex drive is not so much a force of interpersonal encounter, but rather, as William H. Masters calls it, "a completely egocentric matter." This amounts to recognizing in sexual pleasure an essentially auto-erotic dimension. Following his comparison with the morals codified in the past, Béjin recalls that masturbation is the "new canonical sexual act." In the egocentric perspective set in place by the technicians of mating, intercourse is not "communion" but "a series of acts of communication" leading to "two solitary pleasures" or "a climax of two egoisms."[29] One might note here as well the contention of the historians of masturbation,

Anne van Neck and Jean Stengers, that the medical prohibition of the nineteenth century has been replaced by the instruction to masturbate, now part of the code of good conduct elaborated by the theoreticians of the sexual revolution.[30]

In the critical sociology of contemporary sexuality, no one has better captured the dynamic relations between religion and sexuality than Abdelwahab Bouhdiba. His *La sexualité en Islam*[31] treats modernity in the Arab-Islamic countries not as a liberating change but as a crisis of meaning, of human values, of faith. In the Muslim system of belief, there existed a series of prohibitions recognized not as constraints but as requirements for human development. But the traditional ethical ideal gave way to a quick sexuality, "brief and joyless." In desacralizing sexuality, the countries of northwest Africa threw themselves into an "ethical void" dominated by "sexual idiocy, studied childishness." The partner is not subject but object. Stripped of its myths and taboos, sexuality is but an alienating bodily commerce in which the spirit plays no part. Against the dominance of a sexuality seen exclusively as play, Bouhdiba pits a fine dialectic of licit and illicit that gives sexuality positive meaning. His "therapeutic" conclusion is an almost obsessive insistence on rediscovering the meaning of human sexuality. The book is reminiscent of Catholic treatises on the theology of sex.[32]

Unlike their counterparts today, the authors of the traditional codes looked with suspicion on the place of sexuality. This devaluing of pleasure was due, one must admit, to the duty of abstinence of Catholic priests. When a medieval monk describes woman as a "sack of bird droppings," one imagines with how much difficulty his own desires were repressed. But all is not negativity in the traditional Catholic theological discourse. The historians have greatly exaggerated the priests' castrating work. Flandrin condemns the proposals of the sixteenth-century theologian, Benedicti: "The husband...must not use his wife as a whore."[33] Is this a condemnation of pleasure or a call for moderation of passion, tempered by the loving *feeling* necessary for life in common? A good many women of the twentieth century would find that Benedicti was not so bad a sexologist, suggesting an integral encounter instead of the simple insertion of penis into vagina. Our generation, possessing Flandrin's kind of historic awareness, has fabricated a caricature of history, the better to legitimate the sexual revolution. We have too easily concluded that religion was synonymous with denial of pleasure and that enjoyment could be gained only at the price of splitting the two apart. It is, of course, out of the question to write a history encouraging return to traditional religious faith. But a minimum of tolerance requires us to disclose that the simple peasants of not so long ago did not pit, as we do, pleasure against faith. Besides, the breathless search for pleasure has not led our contemporaries to any imagined gardens of delight. Before the revolution of chemical contraceptives, a pensive Freud hesitated to attribute unalloyed bliss to a generation that was detaching itself massively from prohibitions. Would medical advances make the possibility of enjoyment still more difficult? Freud's answer is pessimistic:

> What good is it to check infant mortality if precisely this imposes on us severe restraint in procreation and if it turns out that we do not raise more children than back when hygiene did not exist, while on the other hand the conditions of our marital sexuality become complicated and the beneficial action of natural selection is thwarted?[34]

Freud could not foresee, in the thirties, the coming of chemical contraceptives. But they came, ensuring the technical conditions for the revolution in morality that we have enacted. But has distress of sexual origin been eliminated in relaxing the conditions for pleasure? For the obsessive neurosis so characteristic of the first half of the twentieth century there has been substituted a pathology that psychiatrists consider incurable: narcissistic neurosis. Reviewing the recent medical literature, Christopher Lasch describes the narcissist as having not fixations, phobias, or well-defined symptoms derived from converting sexual energy into nervous disorders, but instead a vague dissatisfaction with life, a feeling of futility, purposelessness, emptiness and depression. Psychoanalysis, Lasch observes, had its origin in the treatment of repressed, morally rigid individuals, but now faces patients who do not repress or sublimate but instead "act out" their conflicts, people who substitute sexual promiscuity for repression, but find no satisfaction therein.[35]

To rediscover the meaning of human sexuality in the past—is this not to act as a humanist or moralist? Is it not to offer contemporaries another frame of reference, another way of living the interpersonal relation with sexual content? This look at the past is possible provided we do not limit our observations to the sum of deviations recounted at length in the archives historians investigate. The ample discussion of transgressions expressed just as much a concern for the norm, for the behavioural ideal, as for the frequency of infractions.

I am led to believe that the humanist historical science already exists when I read this quote from Lasch: "Far from regarding the past as a useless encumbrance, I see the past as a political and psychological treasury from which we draw the reserves (not necessarily in the form of 'lessons') that we need to cope with the future."[36] To take lessons from the past has been for two thousand years the humanist calling of history. The discipline's recent integration into the new synchronic, specialized social sciences has banished its mission to the museum of epistemologies.

In *The Culture of Narcissism* Lasch acts as a pioneer of restoration of this former mission, elevating history anew to the rank of philosophy of life:

> "Love," as self-sacrifice or self-abasement, "meaning" as submission to a higher loyalty–these sublimations strike the therapeutic sensibility as intolerably oppressive, offensive to common sense and injurious to personal health and well-being. To liberate humanity from such outmoded ideas of love and duty has become the mission of the post-Freudian therapies....[37]

Here Lasch is proposing the moral requirement, in contrast to our obsession with "constraint." He is suggesting the goodness of altruism as a rule of life, personal unfolding in the creative tension and worry of reaching for an ideal. He is clearing the name of that morality deemed "coercive," disparaged by the theoreticians of western consumer hedonism.

In his quest for a *not*-value-free social science, Lasch is by no means alone. A U.S.-wide inquiry into values led by sociologist Robert Bellah questions the new "therapeutic" morality. The research team aimed at a renewed social science rooted in the tradition of nineteenth-century socio-philosophical essays. In my view, a humanist social science is perhaps what Bellah calls social science as public philosophy–knowledge that accepts its dependence on nonacademic communities, that is available and helpful to those communities, and that seeks to engage them in dialogue. Social science as public philosophy

> brings the traditions, ideals, and aspirations of society into juxtaposition with its present reality. It holds up a mirror to society.[38]

NOTES

This chapter, including quotations herein from the cited French-language editions, has been translated by the editor.

1. Montreal: Harvest House, 1985.
2. In *Man and His Past* (Montreal: Harvest House, 1982) and *Quebec and Its Historians, 1840-1920* (Montreal: Harvest House, 1982), I was not concerned with probing the scientific character of historical discourse.
3. See his *L'anthropologie en l'absence de l'homme* (Paris: Presses universitaires de France, 1981).
4. I have offered a general survey of the undertaking in "Morales d'aujourd'hui, morales d'hier," in Benoit Lacroix and Jean Simard, eds., *Religion populaire, religion de clercs* (Québec: Institut québecois de recherches sur la culture, 1984), pp. 79-94.
5. *Le chevalier, la femme et le prêtre* (Paris: Hachette, 1981).
6. Yves Ledure, *Nietzsche et la religion de l'incroyance* (Paris: Desclée, 1973), p. 23.

7. The quotations are from his *Par delà bien et mal, Prélude d'une philosophie de l'avenir* (Paris: Gallimard, 1966), pp. 65-75.

8. This influence has been noted by Jean-Claude Dussault in his *Pour une civilisation du plaisir* (Montreál: Editions du Jour, 1968), p. 68.

9. See André Burguière, "De Malthus à Max Weber: le mariage tardif et l'esprit d'entre-prise," *Annales* (juillet-octobre 1972), pp. 1128-1138. Burguière maintains that late marriage was preceded by abstinence (p. 1137). See also Pierre Chaunu, *Un futur sans avenir–histoire et population* (Paris: Calmann-Lévy 1979), especially Ch. 11.

10. See Solé's *L'amour en Occident à l'époque moderne* (Paris: Albin Michel, 1976) and Fland-rin's *Le sexe et l'Occident* (Paris: Seuil, 1981).

11. Flandrin, p. 254.

12. *Familles, parenté, maison, sexualité dans l'ancienne société* (Paris: Hachette, 1976), p. 198. x13

13. See, for example, Ch. 14 of *Le sexe et l'Occident.*

14. On the second sexual revolution (Shorter speaks incorrectly of a revolution in senti-ment), see Edward Shorter, *The Making of the Modern Family* (New York: Basic, 1975), especially Ch. 3. In the work cited above, Chaunu has recounted, not without emotion, the genesis of this revolution.

15. Wilhelm Reich, *La révolution sexuelle* (Paris: Christian Bourgeois, 1982), p. 32.

16. See Reich, pp. 54f, 63, 67.

17. *Ibid.*, pp. 71-74.

18. "Réflexions sur l'histoire de l'homosexualité," *Communications*, No. 35 (Paris: Seuil, 1982), p. 62.

19. *Histoire de la sexualité*, volumes 2 and 3 (Paris: Gallimard, 1984).

20. *L'amour en Occident à l'époque moderne* (Paris: Albin Michel, 1976).

21. *Le pénis ou la démoralisation de l'Occident* (Paris: Grasset, 1978).

22. Paris: Seuil, 1984.

23. See, in this connection, Henri-Irénée Marrou, in Jean-Marie Mayeur, ed., *Crise de notre temps et réflexion chrétienne* (Paris: Beauchesne, 1978), pp. 450f.

24. On the history of sin and its acknowledgement, see Jean Delumeau, *Le péché et la peur–la culpabilisation en Occident XIIIe-XVIIIe siècles* (Paris: Fayard, n.d.). The best of recent works remains the collection of the Bussiére Group, *Pratiques de la confession–des pères du désert à Vatican II* (Paris: Cerf, 1983). These works approach the history of confession as progression to which one consents, as a healing and voluntary humbling of oneself. Donzelot and Foucault have highlighted the call to confession. For the former, see *La police des familles* (Paris: Minuit, 1977), Ch. 5. For the latter, see *Histoire de la sexualité*, Volume 1, *La volonté de savoir* (Paris: Gallimard, 1976). I think the wish to know answers the wish to say. Whether there is or is not a sacramental mechanism of confession hardly changes the essential problem. The Bible brims with passages on sin and forgiveness. Our twentieth century, opposing freedom to repression instead of joining it to responsibility, cannot understand the ideas of sin, regret, and atonement. Techniques of justification, by contrast, whether by individuals (rationalizations) or by collectivities (ideologies), aim to shift the responsibility for failure onto other people or onto "the system." On references to sin in the Bible, see Henri-Irénée Marrou, pp. 450-52.

25. Montréal: Léméac, 1972.

26. Marcel Boisvert, "Il faut réhabiliter le sens de la mort," *Le Devoir* (9 novembre 1985), p. 11.

27. "Amours interdites et misères conjugales au Québec: l'arbitrage des prêtres, fin XVIIIe siècle à c1830," in Francois Lebrun et Normand Séguin, *Sociétés villageoises et rapports ville-campagne au Québec et dans la France de l'Ouest XVIIe-XXe Siècles* (Trois Rivières: Centre de recherche en Etudes québecoises, 1987).

28. As quoted in André Guindon, *The Sexual Language: an Essay in Moral Theology* (Ottawa: University of Ottawa Press, 1976), p. 19.

29. André Béjins, "Le pouvoir des sexologues et la démocratie sexuelle," *Communications*, No. 35 (Paris: Seuil, 1982), pp. 178-191. In another article in the same issue ("Crépus-cule des psychanalystes, matin des sexologues"), Béjin defines the sex therapist as a "programmer" whose ethical position reflects the duty of orgasm.

30. *Histoire d'une grande peur: la masturbation.* Bruxelles: Editions de l'université de Bruxelles, 1984.
31. Paris: Presses universitaires de France, 1975.
32. The two that I have read are Guy Durand, *Sexualité et foi–synthèse de théologie morale* (Montréal: Fides, 1977) and André Guindon, *op. cit.*
33. Quoted in Flandrin, *Le sexe et l'Occident,* p. 118.
34. *Malaise dans la civilisation* (Paris: Presses universitaires de France, 1971; first published in l929), pp. 35f.
35. *The Culture of Narcissism* (New York: Warner Books, 1979), p. 60f.
36. Lasch, p. 25.
37. Lasch, p. 43.
38. *Habits of the Heart* (Berkeley: University of California Press, 1985), p. 301. See also Norma Haan *et al., Social Science as Moral Inquiry* (New York: Columbia University Press, 1983), and William M. Sullivan, *Reconstructing Public Philosophy* (Berkeley: University of California Press, 1982).

Part III

PRACTICALITY

7

SOCIAL SCIENCES, HUMAN SURVIVAL, DEVELOPMENT AND LIBERATION

David G. Gil

In this essay, I will develop a tentative set of principles and an agenda for the social sciences from a humanist perspective. Such a perspective implies unconditional respect for every human being, rooted in egalitarian, libertarian, and democratic values, and a corresponding political philosophy according to which humans are, in spite of their individual differences, equals in intrinsic worth and entitled to equal rights and responsibilities in every domain of social life. Humanism involves an unequivocal commitment to human survival, development, and liberation, the underlying themes of this essay.

Principles for social sciences will be derived here from certain fundamental aspects of the human condition in nature and from the related proposition that every moment of human existence, social relations, and interactions involves, inevitably, political and value dimensions. As a societal process, the practice of social sciences involves political and value dimensions and is thus a political act–whether or not social scientists intend it to be that way.

The notion that social sciences could and should be practiced in a value-free manner has by now been rejected by many scholars. The related notion, however, that social scientists could and should be politically neutral when practicing their scholarly disciplines, is often taken for granted even now. This notion requires critical scrutiny.

The Meaning of "Political"

Before discussing aspects of the human condition relevant to the formulation of social-science principles, it seems necessary to clarify the meaning of the term "political" as used here. I am using this term not in the conventional narrow sense of electoral, party, and interest-group politics, but in a comprehensive, dynamic sense. In this sense, *political refers to conscious and intentional, as well as unconscious and unintentional acts or inactions by individuals and groups, which affect established patterns and conditions of life in society either by reproducing and perpetuating these patterns or by challenging them and promoting transformations in them.*

When the term *political* is used in this comprehensive, dynamic sense, political neutrality turns out to be an impossibility for people living and acting in an established society–this includes scholars who study it. Every human action and thought in such an established context will either conform to, reproduce, reinforce and validate the status quo of pre-existing patterns and conditions of life, or will confront, challenge and subvert prevailing social organization and consciousness. Political neutrality is possible only in a hypothetical situation of total absence of societal patterns, such as Rawls's "veil of ignorance" context.[1]

Efforts to remain politically neutral and to depoliticize the practice of the social sciences are actually subtle political acts, albeit unconscious and unintentional ones. Such efforts inevitably promote conformity and non-resistance to the prevailing social orders that "neutral" scholars have chosen not to challenge. Christ, as quoted in the Gospel, seems to have understood the impossibility of political neutrality when he told his disciples: "For he that is not against us, is for us" (Luke 9:50).

The Political Nature of Values and Morals

Once the term *political* is understood comprehensively and dynamically, the essentially political nature of societal values and morals becomes evident. For values and morals are products of social processes rather than politically neutral absolutes derived from extra-human sources. They are guides for socially expected, "valued" consciousness, behaviour, and social relations. Their usual consequence or "function" is to induce consciousness, actions, and relations compatible with the reproduction of established patterns of social life, and to prevent consciousness, actions, and relations which threaten, subvert, and transform established patterns. Analogously, "alternative" values and morals are advocated and practiced by individuals and social groups whose aim is to bring about changes in consciousness, behaviour, and relations conducive to transformations of established patterns of life.

Values and morals are always rooted in and reflective of important needs and interests either of all members of a society or of certain social groups or classes. Thus the value of the sanctity of life expressed by the ancient commandment, "Thou shalt not kill," clearly represents a universal human need and interest. On the other hand, patriarchal values and morals which prescribe preferential status and treatment for boys and men, represent the interests of a privileged, dominant segment of society. Similarly, racist values promote differential rights, responsibilities, and treatment for different racial and ethnic groups, and thus represent divided and factional rather than universal interests. Values and morals concerning the sanctity of property derive from the interests of propertied segments of societies. Whenever property is distributed unequally and unfairly, these values and morals serve mainly the interests of privileged classes.

The political importance of values and morals is largely due to the fact that, in the course of socialization, values which serve the interests of dominant and privileged classes, tend to be internalized into the consciousness not only of these classes, but also of dominated and deprived classes. Consequently, the consciousness, behaviours, and relations of all societal groups tend to conform more or less to patterns of life which reproduce the status quo, and which serve the interests of dominant and privileged groups while hurting, in direct and subtle ways, the interests of other groups in society.

The essentially political nature and consequences of values and morals indicated by this analysis, means that implicit in a rejection of the possibility of value-free practice of social sciences is also a rejection of the possibility of politically neutral practice. Hence, social scientists who reject only the possibility of value-free practice, but not of politically-neutral practice, may be enacting a new variation on the conventional theme of avoiding explicit political challenges to the social status quo. Such scholars may actually protect and preserve their academic standing and respectability when asserting commitments to values as abstractions, rather than as political acts.

Aspects of the Human Condition Underlying the Political Nature of Life in Society and of the Social Sciences

Humans share with other species biological tendencies to survive and propagate, and to unfold spontaneously their innate potential when living in environments in which they can realize their basic needs. Basic needs of humans include, however, not only biological, but also psychological, social, security, spiritual, and creative-productive needs.[2] As to the environment, it consists for humans not only of the natural setting, but also of a human-originated and evolved socio-cultural context. It follows that, while humans share major biological tendencies with other species, their basic needs and environmental requirements seem more complex.

In biological terms, humans seem less adequately prepared for survival than other species, since genetically, they may be the "least programmed" species. Also, as with many species, human offspring are immature at birth and totally dependent on care and support from adults for an extended period. Being genetically less programmed does not mean that human existence is not genetically circumscribed. It means merely that human genes determine only ranges and limits for behaviour, within which humans must make choices when developing patterns for their lives and social relations. Their genes do not determine and transmit specifications for patterns of life and behaviour as the genes of other species seem to do to a far larger extent.

As a consequence of the relative absence of genetic specifications and the immaturity of their offspring at birth, *humans survive as individuals and species only when they create for themselves relatively stable patterns of existence within genetically evolved limits, including systems of care and socialization for their young, conducive to maturation and to integration into established existential designs.* Human existential patterns and social organization are, therefore, ordained by neither biology nor extra-human forces. Rather they are historical products of interactions among individuals, social groups, and natural environments. Societal processes evolved thus into substitutes for genetically specified patterns of life. This circumstance of the human condition–*the existential imperative to create patterns of social life*–is the source of the inevitability of political processes in human societies, aimed at re-creating, maintaining, or transforming human-evolved patterns of social life.

As genetic specifications declined in the course of biological evolution, the capacity for mental processes and consciousness of the nervous system and the brain seems to have increased, making possible the eventual substitution of socio-cultural programming for genetic programming. Mental capacities and processes are thus a product of biological evolution, as well as the medium for and ongoing product of socio-cultural evolution.

The evolutionary shift from genetic specificity toward genetic openness has had important consequences for the political dimension of human life. On the positive side, the human species became relatively flexible to adapt to diverse and changing environmental contexts all over the globe. On the other hand, lacking a pattern of life tested and finely tuned by biological evolution, the human species is constantly faced with the risk of creating, transmitting, and perpetuating patterns of life which are less than optimal in terms of survival, development and meeting basic needs of all members of societies. This risk was certainly not negligible in the context in which human groups took their early steps toward creating patterns of social organization. This early context involved pervasive ignorance of life, nature, human nature, and the universe; limited technological capacity and skills; and a deep sense of insecurity due to precarious conditions of life. It is not surprising, therefore, that existential patterns, once evolved by trial and error, tended to be preserved and reproduced, provided they proved to be minimally adequate.

Human societies seem to have developed strong conservative tendencies to hold on to established ways of life since early stages of social
evolution. Several social-psychological factors may account for this
tendency: a sense of security derived from familiar patterns which seem
somehow to work and to satisfy perceived needs and interests of people;
intense fear of the unknown and of untried, alternative approaches to
existential problems; comprehensive ignorance and limited experience
and skills; habit and inertia; and an apparent tendency to deal with
perceived problems as isolated fragments, by small, incremental steps,
rather than by re-examining the entire societal context from which the
problems arise and readjusting that context in order to prevent the
problems at their sources.

The conservative tendencies of human societies seem also to emerge
from interactions of biological, social and psychological factors inherent
in the physical and mental immaturity, the economic and emotional
dependence, and the limited capacity for critical reflection and
consciousness of children, during stages of life when they are socialized
into and absorb the established ways of life and the dominant values and
ideologies of their societies.

Yet in spite of strong conservative tendencies in human societies, societal patterns, values and ideologies have never been static, but have
always undergone changes, usually gradually, but often also at acceler-
ated rates. While these changes result from various internal and external
societal forces and also from environmental factors, the role played in
social change by critical reflection and consciousness on the part of individuals and groups within societies is of special importance in this discussion of political and value dimensions of social life and of the social
sciences.

A Unitary Concept of Science Derived from the Human Condition

As a human function, science originated in the just described aspects of
the human condition, which underlie the existential imperative to create
viable patterns for social organization. Science appears thus to be a
"twin" of the political dimension of human life which, as noted above,
also derives from that existential imperative.

In a fundamental sense, science is an ongoing, multi-dimensional
process–the entire array of explorations, discoveries and inventions by
which humans strive to orient themselves to the world and to gain some
control over their existence and environment, as they create, maintain
or transform the patterns of their societies. The products of the diverse
processes of science include consciousness of self, others, society and the
human species; of social relations and relations to the environment; of

nature, the supernatural and the universe; of life and death; of time, space and history; and of origins and destination. This generic concept of science includes not only the natural and social sciences but also mythology, religion, ideology, philosophy, art and literature. Implicit in this broad concept is the notion that there are no precise, qualitative boundaries between these different human approaches to gaining consciousness of and comprehending the world. For these approaches are overlapping and complementary stages, dimensions, and media of a unitary process which is intrinsic to, and shaped by, the aspects of the human condition sketched above: the drive to survive, the dynamics of meeting basic human needs, the relative lack of genetic specifications for human existence, the compensatory biological capacity for mental activity and consciousness, and the inescapable necessity to create patterns for social life.

While science as a process and product of consciousness-generating mental activity originated in the human condition, and is shaped and reshaped by the intrinsic imperatives of that condition and the human interest in satisfying real and perceived needs, it has gradually evolved into a substantial force toward creating, maintaining, interpreting and justifying patterns of social existence. However, science can also become a source and means for critical consciousness and transformative practice concerning established patterns of life, when these patterns fail to satisfy basic human needs.

Stages of the Political Orientation of Science

Throughout history, the goals and practice of science were shaped, directly or indirectly, by experienced and perceived needs, the satisfaction of which has always been a key human interest. Implicit in the relationship of science to needs and interests is a fundamental political question: Whose needs and interests are being served by scientific activity in different societies during different times?

During early stages of social evolution, humans tended to live in small, relatively egalitarian communities of hunters and gatherers which were organized to meet everyone's basic needs as far as was possible in the context of limited knowledge and technology. People in such communities therefore had shared interests and their "scientific practices" were consequently conducive to meeting everyone's needs and interests. Clearly, to the extent to which, and as long as, such "classless" and relatively conflict-free communities existed, scientific achievements benefited everyone fairly equally. The political dimension of science at that stage of social evolution may be considered egalitarian and humanistic, since it facilitated and justified the maintenance and perpetuation of ways of life which satisfied the needs and interests of everyone.

As population growth led, some ten to twenty thousand years ago, to gradual transformations of small communities into larger societies, to the discovery and development of agriculture and early technologies, and to social differentiations based on age, sex, origin, occupation, and residence, inegalitarian societal patterns were introduced coercively into earlier egalitarian settings. These new societal patterns had to be maintained by physical force and ideological indoctrination. They involved domination, exploitation and oppression of various groups and classes within societies, and often also wars with and conquests of other societies.

Once societies were no longer organized to satisfy the basic human needs and interests of all their members, and large population segments were forced to serve the needs and interests of dominant, privileged elites, the practice of science also came to be dominated largely by those same elites and was adapted to serve their interests. The political dimension of science in this new context had shifted toward an inegalitarian and elitist orientation geared to the perpetuation of exploitative patterns of life.

The transformation of egalitarian, cooperative, small communities into inegalitarian, exploitative, larger societies, and the related transformation of humanistic, egalitarian science, which served everyone's interests, into oppressive, inegalitarian science, which served mainly the interests of dominant, oppressive elites, has also resulted in the gradual emergence of a counter-establishment, emancipatory science. This alternative tendency in science evolved from efforts of oppressed and exploited individuals and groups and their allies from other social groups, to reflect on their conditions and make sense out of their lives; to orient themselves to their world and comprehend it in order to regain control over their lives; and to develop critical consciousness concerning the dynamics of their situation and the requirements of liberation.

Principles and Agenda for Humanist Social Sciences

Now that politics, values, and sciences have been traced to their sources in fundamental aspects of the human condition, a tentative set of principles and a related, general agenda for humanist social sciences can be suggested.

1. A key principle derives from the realization that social sciences involve, inevitably, political and value positions favouring either preservation or change of established ways of life and social relations. Social scientists should, therefore, choose consciously and re-examine continuously, political and value positions for their practice and theory. In doing

so, it seems preferable to specify positions not as abstract concepts and labels but in terms of desired human conditions and outcomes.

2. It is not enough merely to choose and re-examine political value positions. Rather, chosen positions ought to be integrated consciously into every aspect and stage of scholarly practice: agenda, methods and designs, human relations, teaching, communications, and publications. Furthermore, it is necessary to resist involvement in projects which conflict with one's politics and values.

3. From a humanist political perspective, *the social sciences should facilitate changes of social orders which inhibit the realization of basic human needs and thus obstruct human development, toward alternative orders whose institutions, values, and dynamics would be conducive to the full development or self-actualization of every human being.* This humanist political perspective derives from the above analysis of the human condition, according to which people tend to develop and to unfold their innate potential spontaneously when living in natural and socially-evolved environments in which they can realize their basic needs. To facilitate transformations of development-inhibiting into development-conducive environments, should be the central mission of humanist social sciences.

4. The humanist political perspective sketched here implies the following themes as key components of a social-science agenda:

(a)   roots, dynamics, history, and present context of development-obstructing patterns of social life, in any culture and any part of the world;

(b)   actual patterns of social life, past and present, in any culture and country, and theoretical models of possible future patterns of social life, conducive to realization of basic human needs and to unobstructed human development;

(c)   forces and processes which inhibit consciousness and understanding of the essence of social reality, with attention to the role of conventional, mainstream social sciences;

(d)   models of education and communication oriented toward overcoming forces and processes which inhibit consciousness and understanding of the essence of social reality, and toward facilitating the emergence of critical consciousness;

(e)   political strategies and social movements oriented toward transforming development-obstructing institutions, values and consciousness into development-conducive alternatives. This theme should involve not only theoretical study but also active involvement by humanist scholars in political practice oriented toward human liberation, social justice, and equality.

5. The relationship of scholars to people involved in study projects should be free of all forms of domination, manipulation, and exploitation. People should be considered and treated as autonomous subjects

rather than as objects and "guinea pigs." This principle derives from the humanistic premise that all people are to be regarded as equals in intrinsic worth and dignity. In concrete terms, this attitude towards people requires that decisions on the goals, foci, questions, methods, designs, and reports of a study should not be made by scholars alone, but by all people involved in the study or their representatives, in cooperation and consultation with the investigators. This requirement goes far beyond the conventional "informed consent" concept. Such participation in shaping and controlling social science investigations is likely to enhance the interest and motivation of people involved in them, and should therefore strengthen the quality of studies. It also seems appropriate to compensate people involved in studies for time and effort contributed by them, rather than expect them to volunteer their contributions. As long as scholars are paid for their work in a scientific project, the work of other participants ought to be acknowledged in the same currency.

6. Methods and designs ought to follow logically from the nature of the studies and the question to be explored. As there are no universally valid methodologies and designs for the study of social issues, every study, question, and context is likely to require specific combinations of research approaches. Controversies concerning quantitative vs. qualitative approaches, large sample surveys vs. intensive case studies, empirical-positivist vs. alternative epistemologies, etc., seem therefore to raise false issues, as any of these modes of inquiry may be appropriate for different studies, contexts, and purposes.

7. Considerations of validity, reliability, precision, and the overall level of scholarly competence are not less important for humanist than for conventional, mainstream social sciences. These considerations are necessary to assure the integrity of social science projects, and integrity is certainly a key requirement of a humanist approach.

8. Integrity is, however, not merely a matter of research technology, but is intimately related to political and value dimensions. Consequently, a study could not pass the test of integrity when its substance and/or procedures are in conflict with or irrelevant to the humanist perspective, even though the method and design of the study are valid, reliable, precise, of high quality, and in general, reflective of scholarly sophistication and competence. Thus, for instance, studies of the effects of hunger, homelessness, poverty, and discrimination on human development seem to lack integrity, for these conditions are unacceptable on moral and political grounds, and ought to be abolished through political practice, irrespective of their scientifically measured consequences. Such studies are often conducted not to guide policy, but to delay and avoid action on what is already well known. Such studies are also often undertaken to further the economic interests of research institutes, universi-

ties, and scholars. From a humanist perspective, studies of this type should be shunned because of their amoral, or even immoral, quality.

9. When writing and publishing their scholarly work and findings, humanist social scientists should avoid the use of professional jargon with which only select groups are familiar. Instead they should write in as clear, concise, and simple a style and language as possible. This does not mean that scholars should not present and explain the complex nature of social phenomena they have studied. It only means that substantive complexity should not be made more difficult to comprehend by the use of unnecessarily complicated language and style.

The historic roots of professional jargons and scholarly style reach back to early processes of social differentiation and elite formation. The purpose of limiting the spread of literacy and of developing separate forms of language and communication for priesthoods, scholars, and dominant social classes, has been to exclude dominated classes from access to knowledge and information which they might use in efforts to liberate themselves from domination and exploitation. Humanist scholars should not participate in perpetuating this tradition through their modes of communication and publication.

10. Teaching is usually a process by which established ways of life, and the values and ideologies underlying them, are transmitted to successive generations of students. It is thus a medium for shaping the consciousness of students, but also a potential medium for challenging that consciousness–political acts *par excellence*. The messages of teaching are conveyed cognitively as well as experientially, through substantive content, teaching style, human relations and expressed attitudes.

For social scientists who have come to acknowledge the political and value dimensions of scholarly work, and who have chosen a humanist political philosophy, the classroom and teaching context can become major arenas for political practice toward human liberation. Here they can help students, through a dialogical process free of elements of indoctrination, to develop innate capacities for critical thought and consciousness, to gain penetrating insights into the sources, history and present dynamics of social life, and to develop personal commitment to human liberation and social justice. By practicing the humanist pedagogy of ancient and contemporary philosophers, from Socrates to Martin Buber and Paulo Freire,[3] teachers can consciously transform their classrooms and the entire educational experience into a "liberated space," that is, a counter reality to institutional domination and control, in which students can taste in the here and now prefigurations of possible future patterns of social life and human relations, involving self-direction and freedom in the context of justice and participatory democracy. Teachers choosing this educational philosophy should act as guides, facilitators, and resource persons who respond sensitively and caringly to the evolving motivations and capacities of students, and who refrain consistently from controlling and dominating them through requirements, examinations, and grades.

As to substance, education in humanist social science should involve exploration of the many related dimensions of natural and culturally shaped realities; of what is, what was, and what can be; how all this facilitates and inhibits human development; and how a better fit can be attained between developmental needs of people all over the globe and emerging, human-shaped social realities. The ultimate purpose of humanist education is to facilitate discovery by students of themselves as potentially creative and productive subjects in relation to other individuals, communities, society, nature, and the universe.

Humanist approaches to the social sciences in general and to teaching in particular are likely to conflict with dominant approaches in many contemporary schools and universities, which for many reasons are intimately tied to, and committed to the preservation of the social status quo. Humanist scholars will, therefore, experience tensions, rejection, alienation, and isolation in their places of work, in relations with individual colleagues and with academic departments and institutions. These experiences, which may range from mild to intense levels in different institutions at different times, cannot be avoided when scholars insist on their academic freedom to pursue their chosen political-philosophical course. Constructive responses are possible for dealing with this dilemma, stressing mutual respect, openness and tolerance. One should, however, also realize and acknowledge openly that perfect solutions are not possible. For the conflict is real and serious between majorities who support established ways of life, actively or by implication, and small minorities who are not only committed philosophically to fundamental systemic changes, but also work constantly for transformations of the established social order in line with their philosophy.

11. This dilemma underlies the final principle to be suggested here. Humanist social scientists should be involved actively in social-political liberation movements, on local and translocal levels. Such involvement is necessary and appropriate in personal and political terms, and also to assure scholarly integrity. In a personal sense, involvement in humanist caucuses in workplaces and in scholarly and occupational societies, and also in chapters of political movements is important for mutual support and confirmation of individuals whose alienation is, at least partly, related to their political and philosophical minority status. In a political sense, involvement in organizations and movements is necessary since social change cannot be accomplished without organized, collective practice. Individual efforts in everyday life are, of course, important to promote critical consciousness–a precondition for social transformations. However, individual efforts can only be a necessary complement to

collective action, never a substitute for it. Finally, personal integrity of humanist scholars seems to require their active involvement in political practice for fundamental social change. This necessity was stressed, some 150 years ago, by an important humanist social scientist, Karl Marx, in his apt critique of academic philosophy: *The philosophers have only interpreted the world in various ways; the point, however, is to change it.*[4] Marx's pithy observation on philosophers is equally applicable to social scientists, and in a way summarizes the conclusions of this essay concerning principles for humanist practice conducive to human survival, development and liberation.

NOTES

1. John Rawls, *A Theory of Justice* (Cambridge: Harvard University Press, 1971).
2. Abraham Maslow, *Motivation and Personality*, (New York: Harper and Row, 1954, 1970).
3. Paulo Freire, *Pedagogy of the Oppressed* (New York: Herder & Herder, 1970).
4. Karl Marx, "Theses on Feuerbach, 1845," in Robert C. Tucker, *The Marx-Engels Reader* (New York: Norton, 1978).

8

CAN THERE BE A HUMANIST
SOCIAL SCIENCE?

Shoukry T. Roweis

Critique, as Alvin Gouldner reminded us, is not something one inflicts on an author, a theory, or a body of knowledge. Rather, it is an interrogation of its *sense*: a meditation on its implications and consequences. This expresses tentatively my orientation to both humanism and science.

To Gouldner's dictum I wish to add another, less poetic but still pertinent. The task of critique is *to point out possible dangers* rather than *to expose errors* as such. The latter is not thereby excluded but is made to serve the practical intent implied by the former.

The questions addressed in this paper can be formulated as follows: How compatible are the aims of contemporary science with those of modern humanism? What are the implications and possible consequences of a project whose purpose is to constitute a humanism that is also scientific? And what, if any, are the possible risks and dangers involved in such a project?

My plan is simple. I first seek to characterize contemporary science by tracing some aspects of its recent history. I then examine the relationship between humanism and science, describe some of the recent developments in this relationship, and outline some of the ways in which different groups of contemporary humanists have reacted to the split between humanism and science which emerged around the mid-nineteenth century. This is followed by a description of some of the possible dangers involved in three different strategies by which contemporary humanists have responded to the alleged dehumanizing effects of a growing positivistic orientation in the social sciences. I conclude by highlighting some points raised by this analysis.

Science

How can one describe science without assuming that it is what this or that epistemologist says it is or ought to be, and without turning such a description into a veiled opinion about what one wishes it to be? The outlines of an answer may be given by tracing briefly the historical development of several characteristics of modern science.

Institutionalization

In the West since the mid-eighteenth century, science has been not merely an idea or vision but an instituted activity, an authorized practice. The foundation of the Royal Society of London in 1660 was an early indication of the extent to which some groups of scientists have been able to obtain official endorsement and financial support.[1] By the mid-eighteenth century, "science had arrived; it was an institution, it had acquired its own internal tradition."[2] In America, Benjamin Franklin succeeded in founding the first Philosophical Society in 1743. In France, the great *Encyclopédie des Arts, Science et Métiers* was published in twenty-eight volumes between 1751 and 1772. The *Encyclopédie* is significant in at least two respects.

First, as its title suggests, it exemplified the inclusiveness of eighteenth-century science, which comprised, besides the investigation of physical phenomena, both the pursuit of useful inventions on the one hand, and philosophy, history, and practical discourses on the other hand. We can understand this inclusiveness only by reference to the specific historical conditions under which science was then practiced and to which it responded.

The main task of science throughout the seventeenth century and well into the eighteenth was *to show that a credible alternative existed to the traditional-religious world view of the Middle Ages.* This was undoubtedly one of the aims of the *Encyclopédie.* The project was part and parcel of the far-reaching changes which ultimately took Europe from its prior feudal organization to what was to become full-fledged liberal capitalism. The all-embracing nature of this transition encouraged and made possible a correspondingly inclusive practice of science, wherein the study of history, philosophy, law, or politics was no less scientific than that of astronomy or biology.

But the us Encyclopédie was also an embodiment of an ambiguity within eighteenth-century science regarding the status and legitimacy of speculative and metaphysical thought. On the one hand, there was a growing assault on Catholicism and with it the very basis of theological discourse. Yet on the other hand, it was neither imaginable (conceptually) nor wise (politically) to make a clear break with metaphysics. Science, as Bachelard has graphically put it, "is like a half-renovated city, wherein the new...stands side by side with the old."[3]

Science is also like a city in that it influences and is influenced by the broader conditions around it. When we look at science from the point of view of its institutional history, we see it as *one social practice among others.* Its rules and standards shift. It possesses neither an ideality of its own nor an autonomy that somehow grants it dispensation from the ruptures, discontinuities, even the reversals of history.

Verifiability

Given the history just sketched, science has faced since the seventeenth century the necessity of justifying its claims against numerous objections, resistances, and blockages. If it was to contribute to the struggles against the *ancien régime, it* had to become part of public life. For this reason, it could not shun the concern with common rules of verification. To function effectively, it had to make its results accessible to and verifiable by skeptics who doubted or contested these results. As a discursive rule, verifiability emerged as an earthly necessity imposed by the very bellicosity which gave rise to modern science.

But science did not retain its revolutionary (or at least critical) role for long. A virtual reversal occurred between the 1760s and the 1830s. The heritage of Newton and Locke, Voltaire and Rousseau, gave way to a more limited, and less radical, practice of science.[4] "Science, education, liberal theology, from being fashionable [in the 1760s], had now become dangerous thoughts [in the 1800s]."[5] With the old feudal social relations virtually destroyed, radical criticism of the abuses of the new order was now discouraged. Philosophy and social criticism no longer belonged to science. Thus also began the split within philosophy out of which emerged what were then called the moral sciences.

Intersubjective Communicability

The gradual rise in the importance attached to verifiability and the growing intolerance, within science, of philosophy and the moral sciences reinforced each other. Verifiability of scientific results requires that concepts, propositions, and empirical observations all have *intersubjectively communicable* meanings. A condition allowing any of these to mean different things to different people undercuts the possibility of verification.

In the era of ascendent capitalism, expelling philosophy and the moral sciences enhanced the communicability of scientific results, opened up new possibilities of verifiable experimentation, and understandably added legitimacy to scientific claims. At the same time, advances in methods of observation, experimentation and verification, intensified science's intolerance of the inherent indeterminacy of philosophic and moral terms.

Totalization

In a meticulous account of the "genesis of industrialism and modern science, 1540-1640," John Nef stresses the following as a condition of their possibility: "[m]en had to believe that their minds gave them the capacity to reach judgements that were valid for all creation."[6] As a first approximation, totalization refers to this kind of belief.[7] It is not just another term for generalization. Since the Enlightenment, and at least in the social sciences,[8] totalization came to involve much more than an aspiration to arrive at generalizable conclusions.

The mid-nineteenth century was the heyday of liberal capitalism. Most important initiatives–economic, administrative, political, or military–were now firmly in the hands of the new bourgeoisie. The Revolution of 1830 in France and the Reform Bill of 1832 in Britain ushered in the beginnings of constitutional democracy.[9] The *people*, in whose name the progressives of the 1760s and 1770s had advocated reform and revolution, were now classified as the *masses*, the lower class, the poor, the mob. The liquidation of large feudal estates and the Enclosure Acts only helped to concentrate "the problem of the masses" in the growing cities. In this context, managing and regulating the masses became a high priority.[10] Accordingly, this period witnessed an unprecedented drive to rationalize administrative practices. Institutions of various kinds were also being set up and expanded by government and philanthropic agencies alike: schools, hospitals, clinics, asylums, homes for the senile, workhouses, model dwellings, prisons, and so on.

Schools, hospitals, and so on had existed for centuries, to be sure. They cannot be considered bourgeois inventions. But as Foucault and many others have shown, these nineteenth-century institutions were qualitatively different from their classical counterparts. They now functioned as *disciplinary institutions, as apparatuses of a new, and characteristically modern, mode of social power.*[11] These were (and are) disciplinary institutions in two related senses. As sites of social practices, they are disciplinary in that their aim is to direct, train, instill specific morals and habits, treat, extract obedience and docility, normalize, correct, or punish. They are also disciplinary in the sense of being sites in which various branches of knowledge–disciplines–are constituted, articulated, cross-fertilized, and used. It is necessary to stress the significance of the dual nature of these disciplinary institutions, for by their very constitution, they are at one and the same time fields of power and generators of knowledge.[12]

Historically, this superimposition of power relations and knowledge relations constituted a condition for the emergence of what we now call the social sciences.[13] In a statement entitled "Social Science and Social Control," John Dewey exhibits his typical pragmatic clarity about this point:

> it is a complete error to suppose that efforts at social control depend upon the prior existence of a social science. The reverse is the case.[14]

Against the background of this historically specific and characteristically modern relationship between knowledge and power, we may now isolate several aspects of totalization in the social sciences since the nineteenth century.

(1) *The Insistence on a Societal Essence.* In the social sciences, this takes the form of efforts to draw all related phenomena around a single explanatory or interpretive nexus: a spirit of an era, an essence of a civilization, a societal value system, a determinant in the last instance. What is granted the status of an "essence" at the level of explanation serves as a basis for projecting a unitary trajectory at the level of anticipation. If society has an essence, its future must somehow "grow" out of this essence. Two silent effects follow. In the first place, this aspect of totalization undermines conceptions in which the future is seen as contingent, open-ended, or subject to meaningful discontinuities or reversals. Narrowing down the range of believable future possibilities has obvious functions in the exercise of power. Secondly, if society has an essence, a single path into the future can both be envisaged and promised. This becomes the basis on which the scientist or expert anticipates for humans, prepares them, and leads them towards "their" future.

(2) *The Insistence on the Sovereignty of Consciousness.* This insistence has always been a tacit precondition of the effectiveness of the social sciences. Deterministic or excessively structuralist claims have had remarkably little effect in practice. The insistence on the sovereignty of human consciousness does not necessarily entail a conflation of human agency with the human individual; the former has been variously vested in groups, communities, organizations, classes, and so on. What this aspect of totalization entails, however, is an insistence on attributing the sum total of historical development to the agency of the subject, however defined. History is thereby seen as some kind of self-actualization of humanity–a view that claims to find a transcendental foundation for our knowledge as well as for our social institutions.

In practice, this aspect of totalization serves to "ground" an abstract notion of freedom to act, the latter being a precondition of assigning responsibility and accountability to those upon whom discipline is exercised. In return, disciplinary practices can promise the subject "that everything that has eluded him may be restored to him."[15]

(3) *The Insistence on a Human Nature.* According to this notion, man/woman has an essence, an inherent nature, or an original foundation that is given to consciousness, accessible to it, and evolving. Human differences are acknowledged but not allowed to put in doubt this totalizing *telos.* Some notion of human nature is always present in the discursive practices of disciplinary institutions, and it functions in two related capacities. First, it is used to anchor prescriptive judgments into some Kantian conception of what is universally human. This is accomplished

on the basis of criteria of judgment that are said to be universally applicable. For in practice, non-universality is tantamount to arbitrariness. As Hume would have put it, to select one's own fingers, out of all the fingers in the world, to be preserved at any cost is arbitrary. Second, the notion of an intrinsic human nature makes it possible to "ground" moral principles by appeal to various criteria of "healthy behaviour," "natural development," "maturation," and so on. This *medicalization* permits morality to be used as a basis of numerous disciplinary techniques without appearing to function as an instrument of power.[16]

(4) *The Centralization of Knowledge.* This last aspect of totalization is relatively obvious. It refers to the rules and processes governing the appropriation of modern science: access to bodies of knowledge; the right to speak as a scientist; the authority to insert knowledge into social practices; and so on. In all these regards, it seems safe to say that modern science has so far exhibited a marked tendency towards centralization.

In summary, this analysis suggests that science may be described as a discursive practice which, at least in the West, and since the nineteenth century, has been gradually institutionalized, has emphasized the discursive rules of verifiability and intersubjective communicability, and has exhibited an unmistakable tendency towards totalization whenever and wherever the knowledge it produced was used in social practices.

None of this was inevitable. And if its past is any indication, the future of science may well see important shifts, transformations, or reversals. Science has always had to coexist with other forms of discourse: literature, art, myth, revealed faith, and so on. It has never had a monopoly on truth claims. As much as it has influenced other discourses, it has also been influenced by them. Humanism is clearly one of these discourses, the one whose relationship to science I shall now consider.

Humanism and Science

"Humanism," complained Cassius Keyser, is one of the "great indefinables of our English speech."[17] He was probably right, at least with respect to formal, linguistic, or semantic definition.[18] But he and others have tried nonetheless.[19] Albert Levi captures the distinctiveness of the humanist stance when he writes that it

> is important neither to forget nor to underestimate the moral element in humanism. And this is why I found it most useful...to define it as *the quest for value*.... Humanism...shows itself most strongly in its moral and prophetic vein–as *a recall to moral*

order.[20]

This "recall to moral order," Levi points out, presupposes two basic convictions: that non-arbitrary standards of value can be found; and that humans have the freedom to commit themselves to these values "through an act of will."[21] One can safely take these principles and convictions as basic to humanism. In fact, a careful genealogy of Western humanism since the fourteenth century would most likely show it to have been quite faithful to these principles, in good times and bad.[22] [23]

If humanism is the quest for value by humans who are capable both of finding it and committing themselves to its requisite actions and moral standards, then the question is: Who isn't a humanist? In opposition to what forces, which visions, and whose projects do humanists speak? Historically, what was the "other" to which humanists responded? More specifically, has science been one of humanism's foes?

During the Renaissance, humanism was instrumental in the birth of the "new" sciences.[24] A virtual unity of purpose and outlook between science and humanism continued nearly to the end of the eighteenth century. So much so that Wolf, an historian of science, argued that "perhaps the most adequate designation of it [the eighteenth century] would be the Age of Humanism."[25] Most natural philosophers of the eighteenth century hoped to extract an ethic from natural science. To them, the laws of nature and reason contained moral imperatives. An objective moral science was anything but a contradiction in terms.[26]

But as I indicated before, things changed in the early decades of the nineteenth century. The natural sciences were quickly earning a high status in view of their experimental advances as well as their practical applications. Philosophy was gradually separated from science. In general, discourses which continued to rely on speculation, meditation, and interpretation were now considered different from the sciences.

> It was from this period in the mid-century that the split between
> the humanists and scientists, which is such a feature of our own
> times, first became serious.[27]

One of the most important manifestations (by no means a cause) of these dramatic realignments was the gradual articulation of a particular philosophy of knowledge which in due course acquired the now familiar name of positivism.[28]

Throughout its career–beginning with the formulations of Saint-Simon, August Comte, and Ernst Mach–positivism laboured to develop and defend a number of discursive rules which, for our limited purposes here, can be briefly summarized as follows: (a) science, regardless of the specifics of its objects, must rely on one set of rules (the unity of method doctrine); (b) knowledge is scientific only to the extent that it speaks about objects which have counterparts in observable experience (the cognitivism doctrine); (c) in contrast to the mere description or classification of "facts," science seeks to construct theories from which law-like propositions can be deduced (the doctrine of deductive-nomological explanation); (d) science cannot know the essence or ultimate origin of things (the Kantian distinction between the empirical and the transcendental); and (e) science neither claims nor seeks certainty of knowledge, but must operate on the basis of procedures which allow prompt rectification of errors.

Having briefly described the history and meaning of positivism, let me now return to the question I posed earlier. Has science been one of humanism's foes? The answer is not as simple or as straightforward as is often supposed. One is tempted to think that humanism has always, at least since the mid-nineteenth century, spoken in opposition to positivistic social science, or fashioned itself as an alternative to it. But as I shall suggest, this has not always been the case. Faced with the growing influence of positivist doctrines in the social sciences, humanists adopted at least three distinct strategies. For ease of recall, I shall refer to these respectively as coexistence, separation, and absorption. In the remainder of this section, I shall outline what I take to be the main features of each of these strategies. In the following section, I shall discuss some of the consequences and dangers accompanying each.

The Strategy of Coexistence

Humanists who adopt this strategy seem to realize that science is not what epistemologists say it is; that positivism is no more than a "regime of truth"; that the norms by which it grants or denies scientific status to truth-claiming statements are, to put it mildly, flexible; that the test of scientific-ness occurs in the domain of social practices and not necessarily in the towers of academe; and that what is crucial for a humanist is to be effective in public life. In my view, adherents to this strategy of coexistence include John Stuart Mill, Max Weber, Georg Simmel, Sigmund Freud, Georg Lukacs, John Dewey, Julian Huxley, Pitirim Sorokin, Eric Fromm, Carl Rogers, Abraham Maslow, C. Wright Mills, John Kenneth Galbraith, E. P. Thompson, and Albert Schweitzer. The list is clearly no more than illustrative. Despite important differences in approach, outlook, basic presuppositions, and substantive claims among these humanists, they nonetheless share a recognition of the problems facing the pursuit of knowledge about human phenomena on the one hand, and a commitment to the values of human dignity and freedom on the other hand. Their work has been undeniably effective at least in the sense of influencing broad domains of social practice.

The Strategy of Separation

In contrast, those who adopt the strategy of separation almost invariably start by problematizing the relationship between the natural and the social sciences. The issue is treated ontologically and methodologically. A dichotomy is constructed between explanation (seen as appropriate in the natural sciences) and understanding (seen as the only sensible orientation in the social sciences). The history and details of these debates are relatively familiar.[29] The separation of natural and social sciences is seen as a precondition for developing viable humanistic social inquiries. Because human beings are self-interpreting, the social sciences cannot and should not aspire to an interest-free account of human phenomena.[30]

In opposition to the objectifications of modern science, the subjective or existential element is emphasized. The fragmentation resulting from scientific specialization is countered by a holism that celebrates the indivisibility of human experiences. Questions of method and philosophy predominate.[31] Humanism is seen partly as an act of rebellion against an alienating society whose problems are compounded by a mindless positivism.

Humanists who adopt the strategy of separation rely on the philosophical idealism of Edmund Husserl, Wilhelm Dilthey, and Martin Heidegger, among others. They cite the committed works of authors like Jean-Paul Sartre, Maurice Merleau-Ponty, Herbert Blumer, Alfred Schütz, Peter Berger, Thomas Luckmann, and Harold Garfinkel as "models" of viable efforts to develop a "scientific" humanist alternative to the positivistic social sciences.

The Strategy of Absorption

The inspiration of this strategy has a long history in German philosophy: from Hegel through Feuerbach to Marx down to the Frankfurt School. By far the most prolific and influential member of this School has been Jürgen Habermas. His much celebrated approach, the critical theory of society, has been evolving through a set of mutations over the last twenty-five years. It is clearly beyond possibility here to attempt even a summary of his work. What is necessary, however, is to sketch briefly just two aspects of his work that have had the widest impact on humanistically oriented social scientists and professionals: his theory of knowledge, and his proposal for a dialectical resolution of the *is-ought* problem.

In a nutshell, Habermas posits as quasi-transcendental categories three knowledge-constitutive human interests: prediction and technical control, communicative mutual understanding, and emancipation. To each corresponds a type of knowledge that best serves it. Empirical-analytical knowledge, best codified in the rules of positivism, serves the interests of technical control. If applied to human and social relations, this kind of knowledge leads to a form of technical authoritarianism mediated by science. Hermeneutical knowledge serves the interests of clarification of meaning and mutual understanding. Finally, critical theory serves the interests of emancipation: doing away with historically unnecessary restraints on human freedom.[32]

In essence, Habermas's critique of positivism centres on its pretention to exhaust the domain of all valid knowledge. Interpretive and dialectical reasoning can and should complement empirical-analytical reasoning to create a comprehensive critical theory capable of unifying all three human interests and hence of serving emancipatory goals. Habermas has modified his position on many points related to this theory of knowledge. But the upshot remains the same: a unified critical theory of society must *annex and absorb* current empirical-analytical knowledge as one of its components.[33]

Connected to this unification of knowledge are Habermas's views on the relationship between facts and values. He rejects the self-restricting insistence of positivism that cognitive knowledge cannot guide normative choices. From a complex argument regarding the issue of value neutrality, he concludes that dialectical reasoning can indeed ground normative prescriptions in cognitive knowledge. Hence decisions regarding social goals, determinations of the good life, "can be released from pure arbitrariness and can be legitimized, for their part, dialectically from the objective context." He adds, "only to this extent may we expect scientific orientation in practical action."[34]

Habermas's influence on modern humanism cannot be overemphasized. His continued espousal of Marx's materialism has immunized his work against charges of "bourgeois science." Yet his critique of Marx's exaggerated emphasis on the forces and relations of production has enabled him to generate what has been called a cultural marxism, in which human agency is seen to play a prominent role. In addition, his promise of a critical theory by which prescriptive (or policy) judgments can be justified scientifically, has responded to a long frustrated hope among humanistic professionals. Now, the "recall to moral order" may finally be "grounded" in science. In a sense, the attraction of critical theory is the promise of a modern return to the spirit of the eighteenth century: a life in which science, history, and philosophy act in unison in the service of human emancipation.

To summarize, contemporary humanism has so far seen itself as one of the main voices against what emerged in the mid-nineteeth century as a positivist orientation in the social sciences. Whereas humanists have been nearly unanimous in their opposition to what they regard as the reifying, dehumanizing, and alienating consequences of this positivism, they have adopted different strategies in their efforts to respond to these problems. I have outlined three of these. Although I make no claims that they are exhaustive, I believe that they are the most important. The following section considers briefly some of the possible dangers accompanying each of these strategies.

Dangers

Despite their important differences, the strategies of coexistence, separation, and absorption have two things in common. They all affirm humanism and its belief in the naturalness, goodness, freedom, and perfectibility of humans. But they also want humanism to be scientific–beyond positivism and structuralism, of course, but scientific nonetheless. To all three, we may put these questions:

> Which speaking, discoursing subjects–which subjects of experience and knowledge–do you...want to diminish when you say: "I who conduct this discourse am conducting a scientific discourse, and I am a scientist"? Which theoretical-political *avant garde* do you want to enthrone...?[35]

In directing such questions to the adherents of the three strategies, the aim is not to inflict criticism on them or to join the contests which rage among them, but rather to remind ourselves of the ever present possibility that these strategies may produce effects that we are willing neither to endorse nor to tolerate.

Regarding the Strategy of Coexistence

As we saw, adherents to this strategy do not highlight their epistemological and methodological disagreements with positivism. Their first premises, therefore, appear quite noncontroversial. A concept of human *authenticity* is usually adequate as a point of departure. To be human is to aim for authenticity, to be true to one's self, to seek that which most naturally corresponds to one's inherent potential. It is not just in humanistic psychology that this premise potentiates the scientific activity; humanists in other fields rely on it as well.

Authenticity is then treated as the foundation or springboard for relating to others. The self has the embryo of the social being. It is already endowed with a native, if sometimes dormant, recognition of bonds of mutuality and responsibility. Because the self is *natural*, it can be constituted as an object of scientific analysis. For what is natural is susceptible to systematic research. But insofar as the self is also bound towards authenticity, growth, development, self-actualization, need-fulfillment, bonds of mutuality with others, and so on, it is *good*. In this manner, a link is established in the humanist discourse between what science studies (the natural) and what the results of science can, in practice, prescribe (the good).

It is generally along these or similar lines that adherents to the strategy of coexistence accomplish the crucial, and as I shall argue, *potentially anti-humanist* move from nature (the self or social being as an object of scientific inquiry) via ethics (the kind of relationship authenticity naturally propels a human to form with himself or herself) to morality (the kind of relationship self-fulfillment naturally requires one to establish with others). Thus authorized by a humanist *science*, moral prescriptions may be used in practice. Within the order of power, in the day-to-day seemingly uneventful practices of disciplinary institutions, this kind of humanism provokes little shock. Not only that, but to the extent it is used for long periods of time in schools, clinics, hospitals, and so on, its subsequent scientific observations of humans already "treated" tend gradually and predictably to "confirm" its scientific propositions. In short, this kind of "recall to moral order" functions in two capacities: as an instrument of modern power, and as a self-vindicating discourse. The two capacities reinforce one another.

The main danger facing the strategy of coexistence resides in its vulnerability to most of the aspects of totalization I outlined before. In seeking the status of scientific humanism, it faces in practice, and regardless of the motives of practitioners, the danger of serving not the cause of freedom and autonomy but its opposite.

Regarding the Strategy of Separation

Despite occasional claims that phenomenological or hermeneutical knowledge is or can be scientific,[36] it is difficult to see how such knowledge can meet the conditions of verifiability and intersubjective communicability discussed above. This, of course, is not a criticism. In science, evidence is central and reflection occurs at the periphery, the latter being necessary only when scientific mutations problematize the meanings of familiar concepts. But for the exponent of phenomenology or hermeneutics, it is, as it must be, the other way around; reflection is always at the center since meanings are never given at the outset.

For this reason, the humanistic discourse of phenomenology and hermeneutics is relatively incapable of functioning in the social practices of disciplinary institutions. To this extent, it is immune to the dangers of producing anti-humanistic effects. Yet this immunity is bought at a price, namely, isolation from social practices. If John Dewey is right in maintaining that involvement in such practices is a precondition of viable scientific development, then the adherents to the strategy of separation have little opportunity to develop an evolving body of knowledge.

Regarding the Strategy of Absorption

Throughout its career, critical theory constituted itself as a sustained critique of contemporary capitalism. Professionalism and technocracy have been a central target in this critique. At one point, Habermas described science and technology as ideology, arguing that the pursuit of procedural rationality and technical control threatens to erode the consensual foundations necessary in a truly rational society.[37]

As I indicated above, critical theory seeks to respond to this by proposing a dialectical (as opposed to a formal-logical) grounding of normative judgment in scientific knowledge. In this fashion, cognitive, communicative, and normative claims would all be submitted to the bar of critical theory; a mega-discourse that absorbs not only positive science but hermeneutical and deliberative-political discourses as well.

One must now put Foucault's question to those who adhere to the strategy of absorption: "Which theoretical-political avant garde do you want to enthrone...?" Are you not in danger of investing critical theory and those who uphold it and act as its practitioners with enormous effects of power? If those adherents are now disenchanted with the total-izing effects of professionalism and technocracy, how much more diabolic are things likely to get should a new priesthood of critical theo-rists be authorized, in the name of the "new science," to adjudicate major policy issues?

There is an irony in all of this. Critical theory has always been opposed to science, which it took to mean the same thing as positivist science. And yet the ultimate logic of critical theory is frightfully similar to August Comte's "new religion of humanity," whose priests were to be the social scientists and the rulers of society as well. In the name of a humanist opposition to the totalizing effects of science, those who adhere to the strategy of absorption run the danger of multiplying its dehumanizing effects.

Concluding Remarks

To many, the preceding analysis may appear hopelessly naive if not pointless. It may be said, for example, that a humanist social science already exists and that the question regarding the compatibility between the aims of contemporary humanism and those of modern science is, therefore, meaningless. It is common knowledge that for many marxists (and some non-marxists as well), humanism is almost synonymous with bourgeois social science. And for understandable reasons. Most humanists uphold the totalizing beliefs in a societal essence, in the sovereignty of consciousness, and in the existence of an intrinsic human nature–so much that humanism is often defined by reference to these same beliefs. Furthermore, as I noted in my discussion of the strategy of coexistence, most contemporary "bourgeois" social scientists see no incompatibility between their practices and those of some humanists. Why, then, pose a question whose answer is obvious? May I not be accused of labouring in vain since, practically speaking, the modern social sciences are already saturated with humanist beliefs? I must now respond to these objections.

As I mentioned in my introductory comments on the purposes of critique, my interest in humanism's relationship to science centers on the *possible risks or dangers* associated with projects whose aim is to constitute a contemporary humanism that is also scientific. Such risks, as I argued subsequently, reduce to the possibilities of perpetuating existing forms of dehumanization: objectification of the human subject, techniques of subjugation and domination, experiences wherein humans participate in surrendering their own subjectivity, and so on. From this perspective, to interrogate humanism and science amounts to *questioning their possible dehumanizing effects*. This, it should be said in passing, involves no imputation of motives or master schemes to actual individuals or groups.

In conducting such an analysis, one must not imagine that what is being questioned is the whole of humanism or the whole of science. As we saw, not all aspects of humanist or scientific practices can justifiably be accused of dehumanization. One must therefore isolate those particular aspects (or elements) which may demonstrably be linked to the perpetuation of dehumanizing effects. In turn, this implies a refusal to "epistemologize" the issue of dehumanization. Instead, one focuses the analysis on the *social practices* in which knowledge is deployed and dehumanizing effects produced. By thus interrogating humanism and science in the preceding analysis, a number of points emerged which must be briefly recalled here.

With respect to humanistic practices, I tried to show that the dangers of dehumanization are not linked to the general "quest for value" or to humanism's defense of dignity and freedom as such, but rather to the specific disciplinary and normalizing techniques whereby totalizing beliefs are made to function as grounds for the pseudo-scientific justification of normative choices including moral ones. This is clearly one of the procedures by which modern forms of power produce dehumanizing effects without resorting to visible coercion. And it is a procedure which has often absorbed and deformed humanist aims. None of this is meant as a criticism of morality as such. The "recall to moral order" is an abstraction. Like other abstractions, it produces actual effects only to the extent it is translated into specific social practices. One may therefore conclude that *from a humanist point of view, the risks of perpetuating dehu-*

manizing effects are not linked to humanism as such or even to moralizing as such, but to the Judas-like deployment of particular moral (and other) values, with all the power effects this implies, while feigning–or worse, believing–to be merely acting as a scientist.

In a similar vein, my discussion of modern science questioned the notion, unfortunately still prevalent among contemporary humanists, that science is dehumanizing because it is positivist. This questioning was meant as a reminder that an abstract critique of positivism may well miss its target by failing to draw attention to the dehumanizing effects of scientific totalization. To this, my comments on the strategies of coexistence and absorption were intended to add the cautionary note that nonpositivist "alternatives" are not, by virtue of being nonpositivist, immune to the dangers of totalization, and hence may well reproduce dehumanization. One can therefore say that *it is perhaps not positivism but totalization that permits the use of modern science in dehumanizing practices.* The abstract discursive rules advocated by the former can produce such effects only to the extent they are applied to the beliefs encouraged by the latter.

Now, if it is not humanism *tout court* that may justifiably be accused of perpetuating dehumanizing effects but only this fraudulent form of humanistic morality that lays claim to scientific foundations; and if it is not the *entirety* of science that may be similarly accused but rather its totalizing presuppositions and practices; then what we have today is not a humanist social science but a deformed psuedo-scientific humanism. Thus the question still stands: Can there be a humanist social science?

If we now add that neither humanism nor science exhibits the characteristics of a unitary or closed system; that their history (which is the history of their present) gives ample evidence that both have comprised diverse, loosely related, and sometimes conflicting, discursive elements; and that the same history shows how both witnessed important transformations and even reversals in the course of which some of these elements were purged out; then we can no longer rule out the possibility of qualitative changes in what is now practiced in the name of humanism and/or science. One may safely conclude that the objections I formulated above are unfounded.

Whether the aims of contemporary humanism can be made compatible with the methods and procedures of modern science is ultimately a practical-political issue. Analytical clarification, to which this essay may hopefully contribute, can at best specify the conditions of possibility of a humanist social science. In my view, there are mainly two conditions: we must abandon the humanistic dream (or nightmare) of a scientifically grounded normative discourse, and we must reject the totalizing presuppositions and practices of science.

NOTES

1. See Stephen F. Mason, *A History of the Sciences* (New York: Macmillan, 1962), pp. 253 and 260.
2. John D. Bernal, *Science in History* (London: Watts and Co., 1954), p. 363.
3. Gaston Bachelard, *The New Scientific Spirit* (Boston: Beacon, 1984), p. 7.
4. In the 1790s, it was commonly accepted among the British landowning elite and their allies in parliament and the administration that much of the trouble in the American colonies was due to the influence of "free thinkers" at home and in Europe. See Edward P. Cheyney, "Humanism; Historical Aspects," in *Encyclopedia of the Social Sciences*, ed. Edwin R. A. Seligman (New York: Macmillan, 1932), p. 541. In 1791, rumours that a group of scientists meeting in Birmingham expressed support for the French revolutionaries prompted a mob defending "Church and King" to burn down Joseph Priestly's house, where the gathering took place (Bernal, p. 376). The event symbolizes the changes which were taking place around the turn of the century.
5. Bernal, p. 385.
6. John Nef, *The Conquest of the Material World* (New York: Meridian, 1967), p. 326.
7. The term *totalization* is admittedly obscure. Its full connotations and analytical significance are developed in Michel Foucault's work. In particular, see his *The Archaeology of Knowledge*, tr. A. M. Sheridan Smith (New York: Pantheon, 1972); *Discipline and Punish: The Birth of the Prison*, tr. A. Sharidan (New York: Pantheon, 1977); and *Power/Knowledge; Selected Interviews and Other Writings, 1972-1977*, tr. Colin Gordon, Leo Marshall, John Mepham, and Kate Soper, ed. Colin Gordon (New York: Pantheon, 1980). The following paragraphs specify the relatively limited meanings I attach to the term in the present context.
8. According to Keith Baber, the earliest known use of the term "social science" occurred in 1791–*Condorcet: From Natural Philosophy to Social Mathematics* (Chicago: University of Chicago Press, 1975), pp. 391-395. From here on, I shall drop the term "moral sciences."
9. See Robert MacKenzie, *The Nineteenth Century* (London: Nelson and Sons, 1880), pp. 99-111.
10. See H. G. Wells, *Outline of History* (New York: Garden, 1931), pp. 860-866.
11. See Zygmunt Bauman, *Memories of Class* (London: Routledge and Kegan Paul, 1982); Michel Foucault, *Madness and Civilization; a History of Insanity in the Age of Reason*, tr. R. Howard (London: Tavistock, 1967); *The Birth of the Clinic; an Archaeology of Medical Perception*, tr. A. M. Sheridan Smith (London: Tavistock, 1973); *Discipline and Punish; Power/Knowledge; The History of Sexuality, Volume I: an Introduction*, tr. R. Hurley (New York: Vintage, 1980); Nancy Fraser, "Foucault on Modern Power: Empirical Insights and Normative Confusions," *Praxis International* 1 (1981), pp. 272-287; Jan Goldstein, "Foucault Among the Sociologists; the Disciplines and the History of the Professions," *History and Theory* 23 (1984), pp. 170-192; David Hiley, "Foucault and the Analysis of Power; Political Engagement Without Liberal Hope and Comfort," *Praxis International* 4 (1984), pp. 192-207; Michael Ignatieff, *A Just Measure of Pain: The Penitentiary in the Industrial Revolution, 1750-1850* (New York: Pantheon, 1978); Charles C. Lemert and Garth Gillan, *Michel Foucault; Social Theory and Transgression* (New York: Columbia University Press, 1982); Bill Luckin, "Towards a Social History of Institutionalization," *Social History* 8 (1983), pp. 87-94; Pamela Major-Poetzl, *Michel Foucault's Archaeology of Western Culture* (Sussex: Harvester Press, 1983); Meaghan Morris and Paul Patton, eds., *Michel Foucault: Power, Truth, Strategy* (Sydney: Feral Publications, 1979); Andrew Scull, *Museums of Madness: The Social Organization of Insanity in Nineteenth Century England* (New York: St. Martin's, 1979); Alan Sheridan, *Michel Foucault: The Will to Truth* (New York: Tavistock, 1980); and, Brian Simon, *Studies in the History of Education: 1780-1870* (London: Lawrence and Wishart, 1960).
12. Foucault, *Discipline and Punish*, pp. 184-185.
13. An anonymous reviewer pointed out that this claim may not apply to some branches of knowledge such as classical political economy. An adequate response to this important point would take me far beyond the scope of the present analysis. But a brief comment is in order. For a long time, and even after the publication of Adam Smith's

Wealth of Nations in 1776, political economy was conceived as a discourse of advice to national governments. Inasmuch as it dealt with macro-scale phenomena (e.g., prices, wages, profits, rents, trade, taxation, etc.), it presupposed and addressed the State as *the* agent of action, the "prince" for whose benefit advice was offered. Even when heeded, such advice could not, by virtue of being applied to State policies alone, penetrate the social body and influence the relations of "everyday material life," as Fernand Braudel pointed out in *Capitalism and Material Life, 1400-1800,* tr. Miriam Kochan (Fontana: Weidenfeld and Nicolson, 1973), p. xiii. The transformation of political economy from a discourse of advice to a science that grows and develops *in* social practice had to await the articulation, in the nineteenth century, of power relations onto knowledge relations.

14. John Dewey, *Intelligence in the Modern World,* ed. J. Ratner (New York: Modern Library, 1939), p. 951.
15. Foucault, *The Archaeology,* p. 12.
16. See J. O'Neill, "The Medicalization of Social Control," *Canadian Review of Sociology and Anthropology* 23 (1986), pp. 350-364.
17. *Humanism and Science* (New York: Columbia University Press, 1931), p. 39.
18. Edward Cheyney recognizes that humanism meant different things in different historical periods. See "Humanism...," p. 541.
19. For a systematic review of the various ways in which humanism has been defined, see Irving Babbitt, "Humanism: An Essay at Definition," in *Humanism and America,* ed. Norman Foerster (New York: Farrar and Rinehart, 1930).
20. Albert W. Levi, *Humanism and Politics* (Bloomington: Indiana University Press, 1969), p. 17. Emphasis in the original.
21. Levi, p. 17.
22. See Nicola Abbagnano, "Humanism," in *The Encyclopedia of Philosophy, Volume 4,* ed. Paul Edwards (New York: Macmillan and Free Press, 1967); John Dewey, "What Humanism Means to Me," in *John Dewey: The Later Works, 1925-1953, Volume 5* ed. Jo Ann Boydston (Edwardsville: Southern Illinois University Press, 1984); Corliss Lamont, *The Philosophy of Humanism* (New York: Philosophical Library, 1957); Levi, *Humanism and Politics;* Jacques Maritain, *Integral Humanism: Temporal and Spiritual Problems of a New Christendom* (New York: Charles Scribner's Sons, 1968); Bernard Murchland, *Humanism and Capitalism: A Survey of Thought on Morality* (Washington, D.C.: The American Enterprise Institute, 1984); and J. P. Van Praag, *Foundations of Humanism* (Buffalo, New York: Prometheus, 1982).
23. By focusing attention on these principles, one avoids numerous confusions regarding what is and what is not humanist; confusions which may otherwise arise due to the fact that rivalries, disagreements, and tensions always existed, and continue to exist, among various factions each claiming to defend the true humanism. For example, the unending disputes between theists and atheists would appear as a secondary issue as long as we do not lose sight of the unwaivering agreement between the two camps regarding the perfectibility of humans and the vital importance of moral order. On the dispute between theists and atheists, see Maritain, *Integral Humanism,* vs. Paul Kurtz, *In Defence of Secular Humanism* (Buffalo, New York: Prometheus Books, 1983); and, John Dewey, "What Humanism...," vs. Sidney Hook, *The Quest for Being* (New York: St. Martin's, 1961). On the basic agreement between the two camps, see A. Dondeyne and Paul Kurtz, eds., *Catholic/Humanist Dialogue* (Buffalo, New York: Prometheus, 1972), p. 13; and, Keyser, *Humanism and Science,* pp. 168-170.
24. See Abbagnano, "Humanism," p. 72; and, Keyser, *Humanism and Science,* pp. 103-104.
25. Abraham Wolf, *A History of Science, Technology, and Philosophy in the Eighteenth Century, Volume 1* (New York: Harper and Brothers, 1961), p. 27.
26. See Thomas Hankins, *Science and the Enlightenment* (London: Cambridge University Press, 1985), pp. 3-13; and, John Marks, *Science and the Making of the Modern World* (London: Heinemann, 1983), pp. 103-115.
27. Bernal, p. 399.
28. The beginnings of positivism can be traced back to the seventeenth century. See Walter Simon, "Positivism in Europe to 1900," in *Dictionary of the History of Ideas, Volume 3,* ed. Philip P. Wiener (New York: Charles Scribner's Sons, 1973), p. 532;

and, Nef, *passim*.

29. For a balanced and thorough review, see Richard J. Bernstein, *The Restructuring of Social and Political Theory* (Philadelphia: University of Pennsylvania Press, 1978).

30. See Charles Taylor, "Interpretation and the Sciences of Man," *The Review of Metaphysics* 25 (1971), pp. 3-51; and, "Understanding in the Human Sciences," *The Review of Metaphysics* 34 (1980), pp. 16-36.

31. See Larry Dwyer, "The Alleged Value Neutrality of Economics: An Alternative View," *Journal of Economic Issues* 16 (1982), pp. 75-106; "Value Freedom and the Scope of Economic Inquiry," *American Journal of Economics and Sociology* 42 (1983), pp. 353-368; J. Nicholas Entrikin, "Contemporary Humanism in Geography," *Annals of the Association of American Geographers* 66 (1976), pp. 615-632; George Raymond Geiger, "The Place of Values in Economics," *Journal of Philosophy* 27 (1930), pp. 350-361; and, Aleksander Gella, *Humanism in Sociology* (Washington, D.C.: University Press of America, 1978).

32. Jürgen Habermas, *Knowledge and Human Interests*, tr. Jereme J. Shapiro (Boston: Beacon, 1971), pp. 301-317.

33. See Richard J. Bernstein, *Beyond Objectivism and Relativism* (Philadelphia: University of Pennsylvania Press, 1983), pp. 182-197. A compact but brilliant comparison of Habermas and Foucault is offered in John Rajchman, *Michel Foucault: the Freedom of Philosophy* (New York: Columbia University Press, 1985), pp. 77-93.

34. Jürgen Habermas, "The Analytical Theory of Science and Dialectics," in *The Positivist Dispute in German Sociology*, eds. W. Adorno *et al.* (New York: Harper and Row, 1976), pp. 142-143.

35. Foucault, *Power/knowledge*, p. 85.

36. See T. Kisiel, "Phenomenology as the Science of Science," in *Phenomenology and the Natural Sciences*, eds. T. Kisiel and J. Kockelmans (Evanston: Northwestern University Press, 1970); David Ley, "Social Geography and Social Action," in *Humanistic Geography*, eds. David Ley and Marwyn S. Samuels (Chicago: Maaroufa Press, 1978); and Carl Rogers, "Towards a More Human Science of the Person," *Journal of Humanistic Psychology* 25 (1985), pp. 7-24.

37. Jürgen Habermas, *Toward a Rational Society* (Boston: Beacon, 1970).

APPENDIX: TEN CLASSIC GUIDES

As this book draws to a close, the question is where you go from here. The main answer is to your chosen field of scholarship, to the production of illuminating, liberating words on a topic important to the human community. Like a carpenter, you study principles for doing your work well. Then you go to work, build something somebody will be grateful to receive.

Yet often in the course of your career, you return to the study of principles, reflect on what you have produced so far, read more books about your craft, and reformulate the tenets guiding your own work. This appendix is for the next such occasion. It offers a list of ten key books, some of which you may not yet have read.

The list is hardly exhaustive. If you have found the present volume useful, you will be drawn to other writings by these same authors and to articles and books cited herein. You remain, moreover, ever on the lookout for newly published books that promise understanding of your life's work.

The significance of the list below is that it comes from a survey I made of participants in the conference from which this book itself derives. I asked each to name the three books he or she would recommend to graduate students, as the most essential foundation on which to build a scholarly career. Books published after 1975 were to be excluded, since it is harder to judge the worth of recent publications. Forty-three scholars replied to the survey, nearly all of them senior and more or less trustworthy professors of social science.

Of the 85 books suggested, many were exemplars of our craft, classic analyses of society and history that can be studied with profit as models for contemporary work. These included Karl Marx, *Capital* (Chicago: Charles H. Kerr, 1906-1909; first published 1885-1894), Max Weber, *The Protestant Ethic and the Spirit of Capitalism* (New York: Scribner's, 1958; first published 1904), Emile Durkheim, *The Elementary Forms of the Religious Life* (New York: Macmillan, 1954; first published 1912), Alexis de Tocqueville, *Democracy in America* (New York: Mentor, 1956; first published 1835-40), Sigmund Freud, *Civilization and Its Discontents* (in Volume 22 of The Standard Edition; New York: Macmillan, 1961; first published 1930), Lewis Mumford, *The Culture of Cities* (New York: Harcourt, Brace and World, 1938), Karl Polanyi, *The Great Transformation* (New York: Rinehart, 1944), and John Friedmann, *Retracking America* (Garden City: Doubleday, 1973).

Exemplars like these are indeed worth studying, but they are excluded from the list below. The exemplar most useful to a social scientist is one closely related to his or her own current work—in substantive focus, methodological techniques or theoretical bent. In all these respects, readers of this book vary widely. Even a selection of 50 or 100 exemplars would hardly be enough.

The list below is composed of books that zero in more specifically on social science and offer reasonably practical principles for research, teaching and writing—principles relevant to any subject matter and to diverse theoretical orientations. The seven such books most frequently cited in the survey appear on the list along with three I chose in informal consultation with colleagues, from those cited less frequently. The list, this is to say, both squares with the survey data and reflects my own judgment.

1. Erich Fromm, *Marx's Concept of Man* (New York: Frederick Ungar, 1966). The best introduction to the thought of the most important social scientist of modern times. Includes Tom Bottomore's translation of the 1844 manuscripts.

2. C. Wright Mills, *The Sociological Imagination* (New York: Oxford, 1959). Not just for sociologists, a very practical guide to good craftsmanship in any branch of social science.
3. Karl Mannheim, *Ideology and Utopia* (New York: Harcourt, Brace, and World, 1936). The single most classic work in the sociology of knowledge.
4. Thomas S. Kuhn, *The Structure of Scientific Revolutions* (Chicago: University of Chicago Press, 1962, 1970). An analysis of the history of science that dispels any notion of objectivity and counsels an ethic of responsibility.
5. Peter Berger and Thomas Luckmann, *The Social Construction of Reality* (New York: Doubleday Anchor, 1966). A study of what and how a human being can know. Easier to read than *Ideology and Utopia*.
6. R. G. Collingwood, *The Idea of History* (New York: Oxford, 1956). A history and philosophy of historical thought. Collingwood's "historical imagination" has a lot in common with Mills's sociological one.
7. Peter Winch, *The Idea of a Social Science and its Relation to Philosophy* (London: Routledge and Kegan Paul, 1958). A short and lucid explanation of what you do as a social scientist.
8. Ernest Becker, *The Structure of Evil* (New York: Braziller, 1968). The Pulitzer-prize-winning author's "essay on the unification of the science of man."
9. Abraham Maslow, *The Psychology of Science* (New York: Harper and Row, 1966). A sketch for nonexploitative scholarship.
10. Floyd W. Matson, *The Broken Image: Man, Science, and Society* (New York: Braziller, 1964). A pointed critique of one kind of social science, and a proposal for a better kind.

Should you read old books like these? Should you not rather stay on your field's leading edge, breaking new ground, making new and original contributions to knowledge? Your ideas will indeed be new, new as a flower grown from last year's seed. The ten books above, like the eight chapters of the present book, are good stock from which to raise your hybrid sprouts in the soil and season facing you.

AFTERWORD OF THANKS

Every book is a thrust toward relationship, an author's effort to enliven further his or her ties with other people. The title page is an invitation to meet, signed by whoever's name appears thereon.

Every book is also an outcome of relationship. The ideas belong to the author only in their precise formulation, organization, and style. Their substance belongs to the relationships that have brought the author to his or her present state of mind. It is to this social fact that the "acknowledgements" in a book refer.

The present book springs from a specific relationship, a three-day conference of 160 social scientists in Kitchener-Waterloo, Canada, in May of 1986. Its authors take responsibility for their respective chapters, and I for the overall composition and organization. But each of those 160 people had a hand in shaping this work, however much each of them might disagree with one or another thought expressed. To name just a few of them would risk unfairness to the rest. Let the signatures of them all within the covers of this book be our gesture of acknowledgement and thanks.

It took more than words to bring the conference off: printing, transport, food, accommodation, and so on and on. Especially because this book aims to cultivate the tie of social science to the wider community, its dependence on that tie deserves to be noted here with thanks.

The conference was the first major step toward the centre for humanist social science planned for Waterloo. The city's three universities–St. Jerome's, Waterloo, and Wilfrid Laurier–contributed equally to the conference budget. A sizable grant from the Social Sciences and Humanities Research Council of Canada diminished further the registration fee that had to be asked of the invited participants.

Publication of this book is a further step toward making the centre a reality, and this in two ways. First, this book propagates certain principles for doing social science well. Second, royalties from the sale of it go not to the authors but to the centre's account. As chair of the local organizers, I give sincere thanks to Professors Gergen, MacGregor, Lasch, Tuan, Baum, Gagnon, Gil and Roweis.

Finally, to you, the reader, thanks for turning a stack of paper into an instrument of communication. The other authors and I hope you have found our words helpful to your work and life, and we wish you well in deciding what to do in response.

Kenneth Westhues

Kitchener, Ontario, Canada
March 23, 1987

NOTES ON CONTRIBUTORS

GREGORY BAUM (ThD Fribourg, 1956; hon. degrees, Wilfrid Laurier, others) is Professor of Religious Studies at McGill University. He is the author of *Religion and Alienation* (1975), *The Social Imperative* (1979), *Sociology and Human Destiny* (1980), *Catholics and Canadian Socialism* (1980), and about a dozen other works of theology, history, and social commentary. He is editor of *The Ecumenist*.

SERGE GAGNON (PhD Laval, 1975) is an historian in the Centre for Quebec Studies at the University of Quebec at Trois Rivières. Three of his books are available in English translation: *Man and His Past* (1982), and the two-volume *Quebec and its Historians* (1982 and 1985). He co-edited *L'église et le village au Québec, 1850-1930*, and has written numerous articles both on Quebec church history and on historiography.

KENNETH J. GERGEN (PhD Duke, 1963) is Professor of Psychology at Swarthmore College. He is co-author of *The Self in Social Interaction* (1968), *The Study of Policy Formation* (1968), *Social Psychology* (1981), and author of *The Concept of Self* (1971), *Social Exchange* (1980), *Toward Transformation in Social Knowledge* (1982), among others. He and Mary Gergen co-edited the 1984 collection, *Historical Social Psychology*.

DAVID G. GIL (DSW Pennsylvania, 1963) is Professor of Social Policy in the Heller School at Brandeis University, where he is also Director of the Center for Social Change Practice and Theory. His books include *Violence Against Children* (1970), *Unravelling Social Policy* (1973), *The Challenge of Social Equality* (1976), and *Beyond the Jungle: Essays on Human Possibilities, Social Alternatives, and Radical Practice* (1979).

CHRISTOPHER LASCH (PhD Columbia, 1961; hon. degrees, Bard, Hobart) is Watson Professor and Chair, Department of History, University of Rochester. He is the author of *The New Radicalism in America* (1965), *The Agony of the American Left* (1969), *Haven in a Heartless World* (1977), *The Culture of Narcissism* (1979), *The Minimal Self* (1984), and other works. In protest of corporate capitalism in publishing, he declined the American Book Award in 1980.

DAVID MACGREGOR (PhD London School of Economics, 1978) is Chair of the Department of Sociology, King's College, University of Western Ontario. Earlier he worked in program evaluation for the federal government. His recent writings are in social and political theory. His book, *The Communist Ideal in Hegel and Marx* (1984), won the John Porter Award of the Canadian Sociology and Anthropology Association.

SHOUKRY ROWEIS (PhD Massachusetts Institute of Technology, 1973) is Associate Professor of Planning at the University of Toronto. Trained first as an architect in Egypt, he has published a long series of articles on planning theory.

These appear in *Environment and Planning, Society and Space*, K. R. Cox's volume, *Urbanization and Conflict in Market Societies* (1978), and elsewhere.

YI-FU TUAN (PhD Berkeley, 1957; hon. degree, Waterloo) is Vilas Research Professor of Geography at the University of Wisconsin at Madison. The leading humanist geographer in the United States, he is the author of scores of articles, reviews and books, including *Space and Place* (1977), *Landscapes of Fear* (1980), *Segmented Worlds and Self: Group Life and Individual Consciousness* (1982), and *Dominance and Affection: the Making of Pets* (1984).

KENNETH WESTHUES (PhD Vanderbilt, 1970) is Professor of Sociology at the University of Waterloo. His best-known book is *First Sociology* (1982).